FAITH UN

FAITH UNDER FIRE

HARRY BAGNALL

with
DAVID PORTER

Marshalls

Marshalls Paperbacks
Marshall Morgan & Scott
3 Beggarwood Lane, Basingstoke, Hants., UK.

Copyright © Harry Bagnall and David Porter 1983
First published by Marshall Morgan & Scott 1983

British Library CIP

Porter, David 1945–
  Faith under fire.
  1. Falkland Islands War—Personal narratives
  I. Title   II. Bagnall, Harry
  997.11   F3031

ISBN 0-551-01060-6

Printed in Great Britain by
Hunt Barnard Printing Ltd., Aylesbury, Bucks.

To unknown and unnumbered
friends who prayed for us.

Contents

Foreword

As a member of the Reverend Harry Bagnall's pastoral flock and a fellow-Yorkshireman, it gives me great pleasure to write this short foreword. Harry and Iris beat me to the Falkand Islands by only a short head but, by the time I arrived in February 1980, they were already well settled in and seemed to me to be a permanent feature of the Stanley scene. I could not then and cannot now imagine Stanley and Christ Church Cathedral without them.

It was characteristic of Harry to stay with his flock in Stanley during the Argentine occupation. He and Iris could have left with other expatriates in the first few weeks, when the Argentine airline was still running. Or they could have gone to Camp at any time until a week or two before the British troops closed the ring around Stanley. But they chose to stay in town to give succour and support to all the townsfolk who remained. As one Kelper put it to me after my return, they were like Falkland Islands flightless steamer ducks sitting on a small pond as the huntsmen moved in with their 12-bores from all sides. In his typically modest, sincere and self-effacing way, Harry tells the story of how his faith upheld him in those last unnerving days. Typically, too, he kept his sense of humour.

It is an inspiring story and I commend it to all who have faith or who are seeking faith.

Sir Rex M. Hunt
Civil Commissioner and former Governor,
Falkland Islands

Acknowledgments

In working with Harry Bagnall on this book I have been given generous help by a variety of individuals and organisations. I am especially grateful to the Falklands Office (as it was then) for initial advice and encouragement, Hamish Robertson of the ITN News Service, several serving officers of the Royal Navy (some of whom were on duty off the Falklands during the conflict), and a number of individuals involved in Christian work in Argentina and the Falklands at different times, who have contributed various information. Any faults in the book are not the responsibility of the above sources.

In some cases minor facts given in this book are at variance with other published accounts. In such cases the details have been thoroughly checked and the version contained here, based on direct observation by Harry and Iris Bagnall, is given as a correction to other sources which, it must be said, are often at variance with each other on matters of detail. By the same token very little is included about events outside Port Stanley, except in so far as news came through to Harry and Iris at the time. This is a 'Port Stanley's eye' view of events, not a documentary history of the war as a whole.

This book would not have been possible without the

commitment of the Intercontinental Church Society. I am especially grateful to Don Irving, Janet Berkovic, and Jack Hywel-Davies who effected introductions.

The people who have done most to ensure this book's completion are Harry and Iris themselves, who saw the project consuming more time than expected out of a precious furlough in Britain, and put up with it with very good humour.

Prologue

> Situated in the South Atlantic, the
> Falkland Islands lie about 772 km (480
> miles) north-east of Cape Horn. They
> consist of about 200 islands, the largest
> being East Falkland and West Falkland,
> and their total land area is some 12,173
> sq km (4,700 sq miles).
>
> *Paper No. 152/82/Revised, 'The Falkland
> Islands and Dependencies'. Prepared for the
> Foreign and Commonwealth Office by the
> Central Office of Information, London.*

On the evening of Wednesday 31 March 1982, the
Secretary of Defence, Mr John Nott, arrived at No. 10
Downing Street. He was a tallish man, whose face
habitually relaxed into an expression of vague
apology. That night he was in a hurry. So were the
other ministers and Government advisers who arrived
one after the other over the next hour. The hurriedly-
convened conference called by the Prime Minister
went into immediate session.

The Foreign Secretary, Lord Carrington, had
already been recalled from Israel. An urgent request

was dispatched to the United Nations seeking an immediate emergency meeting of the Security Council. Margaret Thatcher cabled the White House, asking the President of the United States if he would use his personal influence in South America to intervene in the developing crisis.

It took until 8 p.m. the next day, but in the end the President of Argentina agreed to accept a telephone call from the President of the United States. President Reagan urged General Galtieri to change his mind. He gave a number of reasons and argued them forcefully. Galtieri, less fluent in English, used an interpreter to convey his reply. There were no concessions, no promises. At 8.50 the conversation came to an end. The President of the United States looked grim as he reported back to Mrs Thatcher. In Downing Street, it was a quiet, warm evening.

The cable that Governor Rex Hunt received in Port Stanley was unequivocal. Invasion was imminent, the Argentine armada – an aircraft carrier, four destroyers and four landing craft – was heading for the Falkland Islands. At 8.15 Rex Hunt made a statement on Falklands Radio.

> *Good evening. I have an important announcement to make about the state of affairs between the British and Argentine governments over the Falkland Islands dispute . . . I have alerted the Royal Marines and I now ask for all serving or active members of the Falkland Islands Defence Force to report to the drill hall as soon as possible . . . If the Security Council's urging to keep the peace is not heeded by the Argentine government I expect to have to declare a State of Emergency, perhaps before dawn tomorrow . . . I would urge you all to keep calm and keep off the streets.*

After the Governor's statement the radio announcer said that the Station would remain on the air all night, and promised to broadcast any informaton as it became available. Then the interrupted music programme was resumed.

I was restless; I paced around the room. Through the Deanery windows I could see the waters of the harbour, black and slow-moving in the early moonlight. It was a quiet, warm evening in Port Stanley.

1: The Argentines arrive

> I ordered [the Admiral] to leave
> forthwith . . . he tried to take my hand
> . . . I said I didn't shake hands with
> enemies, and I certainly didn't shake
> hands with people who had been trying to
> shoot at me five minutes before.
>
> *His Excellency Rex Hunt, Governor of the*
> *Falkland Islands, on the telephone to*
> *Falkland Islands Radio, early morning*
> *Friday April 2.*

A boat was slowly making its way into the harbour.

I could just see its lights. It had slipped through the narrows and was making its way round, holding to the harbour's far bank. Its grey outline, unidentifiable in the early morning twilight, passed the jetty and approached Government House, about 200 yards from the Deanery though out of my line of sight. It appeared to be some sort of landing craft. As it moved past, sporadic small-arms gunfire broke out from the vicinity of the jetty. The firing continued after the boat had disappeared from view – long bursts of rapid fire interspersed with isolated shots. From time to time a dull, heavy *Wuff!* indicated mortar fire. The invasion had begun in earnest.

It was 6 a.m. I hadn't slept much. The previous evening had been the night for our small weekly Bible study; we only had a few regular attenders at the best of times, but that night, because it was known that an important statement was to be broadcast by the Governor, everybody stayed at home to listen. Iris and I had listened to the broadcast together. When it was over, we looked at each other. There was no need to say much.

The Bible reading 'system' that we follow in our group is to take the passages appointed for the Sunday following each weekly group meeting in the Church of England lectionary. We find it helpful to come to the service having spent some time beforehand looking at those passages and praying together. That night, though Iris and I were the only ones present, we turned as usual to the lessons for the following Sunday: they were from the twenty-ninth chapter of Jeremiah and the twenty-second chapter of Matthew. It was very moving to read the two selections, both chosen and printed in the lectionary long before anybody knew that in April 1983 our islands would be invaded; Jeremiah's encouragement and promise to his conquered countrymen, and Matthew, born of a conquered race himself, recording Jesus's words to the Pharisees about how they should relate to their Roman masters. If we had needed reassurance that we were not entering this new and uncertain period of our lives without God's knowledge and concern, those readings removed our doubts.

We read the passages, and then we prayed together. We had a great deal to pray about. Afterwards we had supper and by ten o'clock – our normal bedtime – we

18

were in bed. Almost immediately, Iris had fallen into a sound sleep. I got up again after an hour and paced quietly around the house, staring through the windows at the moonlit bay and listening to the reports that were now coming through on the radio.

Until the Governor's announcement the previous night, delivered with a sombre gravity that commanded total belief, I hadn't seriously thought that an invasion would ever happen. On March 21st His Excellency had arrived at Evensong uncharacteristically late. He explained to me afterwards that the delay had been because he had had to make an emergency broadcast. A party of scrap merchants had landed illegally on the Falkland Islands Dependency of South Georgia, and had raised the Argentine flag. The situation had rapidly reached stalemate. In the days following, the Governor broadcast regular bulletins on the situation. The day after his first broadcast I sent my regular prayer letter to the Intercontinental Church Society (Intercon), the missionary society I serve, for distribution to our prayer-partners. It contained news and information. We requested prayer for more Christians to come to the Islands to help in the work, prayer support for a number of Christian families in 'Camp' (the rural areas), and prayer for an increased response to our broadcast services. I did not think it worth mentioning the South Georgia incident.

Some of the Islanders thought that the developments in South Georgia meant that serious trouble lay ahead; others saw the whole episode as a piece of sabre-rattling from Buenos Aires. Many thought that the Argentines were too rational to abandon the conference table and try to get what they wanted by force. I had been inclined to agree with them, and like them I was now taken by surprise.

In a few short hours, the eyes of the world had turned towards the South Atlantic – a new experience for us; most people in the West a month before would have been hard put to say in which ocean the Falkland Islands were, let alone their exact location. It was different now. The Argentine armada really was sailing steadily towards the Islands.

His Excellency, as he had promised, broadcast regularly through the night. At half-past midnight he told us that the Argentine government had not responded to demands that their ships be recalled. At 4 a.m. there was a further bulletin; an offer of US mediation had been refused by Buenos Aires. When it became clear that the invaders were not going to turn back, the Governor announced the State of Emergency that he had anticipated. Arrangements were being made to place all Argentines on the Islands under arrest, 'for their own safety'. Watching from my window in the early hours of that morning, I saw a van drive up to the Upland Goose Hotel two houses away from the Deanery, where servicemen and Marines had arrived to take Argentine residents from there into safety. I ventured out of the house for a few minutes and spoke briefly to the people in charge, but returned home almost immediately. One or two people had emerged from the Police Station on the other side of my house and were also watching, but they too went indoors after a short time.

At five I had given up any hope of sleep. That was when I dressed and prowled about the house. An hour later I saw the lights of the ship entering the harbour.

For a few minutes after it disappeared I stood by the window, listening to the sound of the guns. Then I went into the bedroom. Iris was awake, listening to the announcements on the radio through the open door. 'You'd better get dressed,' I said. 'If you're going to meet the enemy you might as well be properly clothed!' I managed a smile. Several fluttering butterflies had somehow found their way into my insides and wouldn't go away.

Iris got up and dressed quickly. We made coffee. Neither of us felt much like eating. I went back to the window. The firing around Government House was louder and more persistent. The radio was playing music, interrupted occasionally by brief announcements from the station manager. In between announcements I paced from window to window. I prayed constantly – brief 'arrow prayers', just calling on the Lord to be present in this new situation and to guide us in it. It was a totally new circumstance. I tried unsuccessfully to think what I as a minister should be doing at such a time. Surely there were actions I ought to be taking, even though we were confined to the house . . . but nothing came to mind, and I continued to watch and listen and pray. It was impossible to relax; I could not sit down for any length of time, much less do anything like read a book.

At 7.10 a.m. Governor Hunt broadcast again. His voice was relayed from a telephone in the studio: earlier attempts to fix up a radio link between Government House and the broadcasting station had been defeated by lack of time, and Rex Hunt simply rang the station on his domestic telephone. His news was grim. Government House was under attack. The Island forces were heavily outnumbered. The Argentine strength there was at least 200 men, and the forces defending were probably no more than forty strong. The Governor was not aware of any British casualties; the Argentines had been forced to retreat several times; but he doubted whether his small garrison of Royal Marines would be able to hold out for much longer.

He broadcast again at 7.30, confirming that Government House had not surrendered. There were ominous reports of armoured cars approaching from the airfield. It seemed that the troops surrounding the Governor's residence were simply waiting for these reinforcements to arrive, rather than risk their lives by attacking too soon. There were also disturbing reports that civilians living in light prefabricated houses were in great danger because the enemy, approaching from the east, here met with resistance from small patrols. Some of these residents, understandably frightened, were telephoning the studio while the fighting was going on.

We knew that it was only a matter of time before the British forces surrendered. In the Deanery because of the State of Emergency we could only guess what was happening, as we listened intently to each exchange of fire at Government House just a few blocks away. But there was only one conclusion to the matter, and we did not think it could be otherwise. The radio continued to bring us information as Patrick Watts, the station announcer, received telephone calls from our neighbours and people living on the edge of Stanley. The military pressure was irresistible. One caller had a six-foot hole blown in his roof and his water tank had been burst by gunfire. People rang to say that they could see Argentine troops taking up positions at the edge of the town; others reported vehicle movement in the streets. The messages from the Governor all told the same story: despite the bravery and the considerable accomplishments of our forces, it was all going one way. Report after report told of new areas of the Islands which had fallen to the invading Argentines: Moody Brook, the Airport, places we knew well were overrun and destroyed. Much worse were the phone calls to the broadcasting studio from residents of Port Stanley, people we knew, friends and neighbours who were ringing in to say that there was heavy firing nearby, or their house had been struck, or some other information equally disturbing. In the Deanery, we really only saw the end of the invasion. These people had seen the troops coming over the hills and through the streets of Port Stanley, and those living at the other end of the town had been near to the heavy fighting around Government House.

At 8.30 the news came of negotiations for a cease-fire. One of the prime negotiators was an Argentine resident of Port Stanley, Vice-Comodoro Hector Gilobert.

Vice-Comodoro Gilobert had lived in Stanley for the past two years and had recently returned after a few months in Buenos Aires. Though I had not seen anything of him since his return to Port Stanley, I knew him quite well from his previous residence, and liked him; we had dined together – he had a charming family – and our conversations had often touched on spiritual matters. Iris had been quite friendly with his wife. He was the manager of LADE, the Argentine Air Force providing services to the South American mainland.

It emerged later that Gilobert had had a hard time convincing the Islanders the previous night, when news broke that an invasion fleet was coming, that as a member of the Argentine armed forces he had known nothing about it – if indeed he hadn't. It had not been possible to find and arrest all the Argentines in Port

23

Stanley in the short space of time since the Governor's announcement, and Gilobert was still free. Whatever his implication in the matter (and there were many people who believed that he had been planted in Port Stanley to make preparations for the invasion), Gilobert showed considerable courage that morning.

His Excellency sent for him when it became clear that surrender was inevitable, to talk to the Argentine commander. Gilobert left the house in which he was staying and, bearing a white flag, made his way to Government House. His fellow-countrymen were not quite sure what was going on and shots were fired. Whatever the truth of the allegations of complicity in the invasion, it took a brave man to face the guns of his fellow-countrymen unarmed.

After some discussion it was announced that a white flag party – consisting of Dick Baker (the Chief Secretary) and Vice-Comodoro Gilobert – would go to meet with the Argentines. They left Government House and walked towards the Town Hall. Iris and I could follow what was happening on the radio; there were no Argentine officers in sight, and a message was sent by the radio station to the Argentine forces asking for a representative to meet the party. In the event, the Argentines took some time to arrive, and in the interval the two men gradually moved in the direction of the Upland Goose Hotel beyond the Deanery. From the Police Station, a few police appeared on the roadside and watched the proceedings. As we watched from the window, we saw the party come into view. Dick Baker was carrying the white flag; the Governor's umbrella with what looked like a net curtain tied to it. They halted in the road near our gate, waiting.

24

So we watched with camera ready, from our grandstand vantage point, the first meeting between Admiral Busser the Argentine Commander-in-Chief, and the Governor's representative, Dick Baker. Three men appeared from the direction of the Upland Goose. There were handshakes and introductions. Gilobert, who made the introductions, was greeted warmly by the Argentines. We could not hear what was being said; had we been able to hear we would not have understood the Spanish. But it was clear that some sort of agreement was being made. After a brief exchange of comments they all went off in the direction of Government House.

As they disappeared, we saw the Argentine soldiers for the first time. Figures in combat dress and steel helmets, their faces blacked, advanced down the road. It was not yet quite daylight. They seemed exaggeratedly cautious, peering behind every fence and under every bush, nervously whirling round at unexpected sounds. They carried various weapons. Shortly afterwards the first armoured landing craft arrived, huge vehicles carrying anything up to fifteen men and loaded with a fair assortment of equipment. They created an enormous din. The first of them trundled past and took up position near the Town Hall. Two or three others followed and lined up behind it. Eventually there were about a dozen of these vehicles there, each with between twelve and fifteen men. I called Iris, and she came and watched with me at the window.

In between the occasional bursts of gunfire and the movements of vehicles in the street, it was very quiet and still outside. The main activity outside the house was now over, and we came away from the window. It was an odd feeling; there wasn't anything one could do or wanted to do. We still had the radio on, and reception was now rather variable because of the comings and goings outside. Iris prepared some breakfast a little after seven o'clock. We ate, but we didn't feel very much interest in food.

'So they've come,' said Iris calmly. She stirred the coffee. 'I wonder what happens next?'

After we had eaten we cleared the breakfast things away, and I took up my observation post at the window again, listening to the distant machine-gun fire alternating with the heavier explosions of mortars and small artillery. Iris set up her spinning wheel. From time to time I turned from the window and watched her intently spinning. She doesn't normally have much time to spin, because there are so many other things to do. She smiled when she saw me watching her. 'I can't settle to do anything else,' she said.

The cease-fire became official soon after 8.30 a.m., and a message was broadcast asking for medical help at the hospital where three Argentine men seriously wounded in the fighting at Government House had been taken. From the kitchen window I watched Alison Bleaney, one of our local doctors, hurrying past accompanied by her husband and child, heading for the hospital building. She was carrying a white flag. The announcement of serious injury was sobering.

'That was Alison,' I called to Iris in the living room.

Iris shook her head. 'It's hard to take it in,' she replied. 'Those are our Marines, they are servicemen we know. And they're fighting a real battle, it's actually happening, and people are getting hurt. It doesn't seem real somehow.' I knew how she felt.

Shortly after the cease-fire was announced, I called

Iris to the window again: we watched as the invaders raised the blue-and-white flag of Argentina on the flagpole of St Mary's, the Roman Catholic Church. The soldiers watching, as it unfurled in the light morning breeze, still seemed to be quite nervous. It was like a moment in a bad film, with everyone over-acting their parts. I glanced at my own flagpole, standing in the Deanery garden. Nobody seemed to have noticed it yet.

At 10.15 the radio station was taken over by the Argentines. We listened in silence to the voice of Patrick Watts, desperately tired now after manning the station continuously through the night:

> Just a minute – just wait there – No, I won't do any-thing until you take that gun out of my back – We have been taken over as expected by the Argentines. They have given me some tapes they want me to play . . .

Argentine voices were muttering in the background. Then silence, followed by a somewhat nonplussed Patrick: 'Well, they've left me on my own now, they've just walked out . . .' At that moment contact was again established by telephone between the studio and Government House. Governor Hunt described the fighting and the subsequent surrender, and advised everybody to keep calm and – for the present – do what the Argentine forces told them to do. Immediately afterwards, the Argentines took the microphone and began issuing instructions. The first thing they broadcast was a recording of the Argentine national anthem.

In a town like Port Stanley, the radio station is at the heart of the community. Falklands Radio was a

27

small, informal, friendly station, full of local information and other community news, interspersed with old radio programmes—comedies, quiz shows and so on—shipped out to us from London. Patrick Watts, who performed a magnificent all-night broadcasting marathon on the night of the invasion, was a versatile, popular broadcaster whose easy style at the microphone concealed a shrewd professionalism and one or two specialist skills; he was an excellent sports reporter, for instance. Also, in the wider, scattered community of the Falklands themselves, the radio was a vital link and a way of keeping contact between the outlying farms and the capital at Port Stanley. There was a sense in which you could have said that the radio station was the unassuming, omnipresent voice of the people of the Islands. The Argentines had taken over our Governor's residence, had seized our airfield, and now had silenced our voice.

They began to issue a series of edicts over the radio, stern lists of instructions read out in clipped military English with a strong Spanish accent. During the morning we learned that General Osvaldo Garcia was the new Military Governor and Commander of Operations. His first communique gave us a foretaste of what was to follow, despite the courteous language in which it was phrased:

At this highly important moment for all of us it is my pleasure to greet the people of the Malvinas and exhort you to co-operate with the new authorities by complying with all of the instructions that will be given through oral and written communiques, in order to facilitate the normal life of the entire population.

A further communique announced that the Governor, his staff, and the British military personnel on the Islands would all be relieved of their duties and deported from the Islands. The implications of this – the removal of all symbols and instruments of British authority from the Falklands – were just beginning to sink in when a third communique, in much tougher language, imposed a house curfew and warned of severe penalties for infringing it. We were told not to leave our houses, and we were informed that shops, pubs, schools and other public buildings would remain closed for the present. Over the next hour or so there were a number of worried phone calls. For example one lady rang the station in some distress: 'But I've got to go and feed my hens,' she explained (her hens were in her back garden). It was a vivid illustration of the way people are resilient to even the most devastating changes in the way things are; the Islands had been invaded, and people were more concerned about keeping things going – worried about whether their hens would starve or whether they would be allowed to collect peat from the peat shed. It put things into perspective!

The official edict made it clear that, friendly greetings from the operational Commander notwithstanding, the Argentines were here in force and here to stay. We were to remain under cover and in no circumstances leave our homes. The edict described in considerable detail the various punishment procedures that would be invoked if any of the Islanders contravened the new regulations. As it turned out, the situation was regularised within an hour or so, but the intention then was to keep civilians from wandering about the streets. The edict commanded that if there was a real problem that meant one *had* to leave the house, something white should be hung in one's window. The passing troops would see it and come to find out what the problem was. It wasn't a bad idea, though I'm not sure whether anybody took it up.

Iris and I moved around the house restlessly. We couldn't concentrate on anything, and whatever we began we left unfinished. From time to time Iris went to her spinning wheel, but then a noise in the street or a distant noise of gunfire would bring us both to the window. The morning passed slowly; it was like being in prison, and we wanted to go out. We were both thinking of people – mainly the old and the sick – who would be terrified at what was happening, and wishing we could be with them. It wasn't even possible to telephone them to ask how they were, because we had been forbidden to use the phone for anything except essential business. Later in the morning, we listened to some of the BBC World Service news broadcasts. Incredibly, there was no official confirmation from London that the invasion had taken place. Eventually Iris said, 'Let's have some lunch.' Neither of us was particularly hungry, but we sat down to eat.

We prayed together. We always do give thanks for our food, but now we had rather more to bring to the Lord; our fears for ourselves, and for other people who were on our minds at that time. We prayed that God's hand would be very firm upon us during the days to come, that we would know what to do and what to say when our neighbours and friends were in need.

As we began to eat, the doorbell rang. We looked at each other in surprise. Who could it be? The curfew was strict; it couldn't be an Islander. 'I'll go,' I said, and went to the door.

2: The first day

A large task force will sail as soon as
preparations are complete.

Statement to the House of Commons by
Prime Minister Margaret Thatcher, April 3.

I opened the door carefully and looked cautiously out
into the sunny street. An extremely distressed
Argentine civilian was standing there.

'I am so sorry!' he said. 'I am so very sorry!' He was
almost in tears. 'What can I say? There is nothing to
say, nothing.' He gulped back a sob, and wiped the
back of his hand across his eyes. 'I want to help you.
There must be things I can do for you. Necessary
things – you tell me, I will do anything.'

I looked at him curiously. I knew him; he was
temporarily a neighbour of mine. He was an employee
of the Argentine company *Gas del Estado*, and had
been working in the Islands for the past few days on
an installation. He was lodging at the Upland Goose.
A year before, he had been living on the Islands, and
Iris and I had got to know him quite well and had
entertained him several times. He was obviously
deeply embarrassed by the events of the morning. He

was speaking with some difficulty.

'Please – tell me what I can do for you.'

I had a sudden idea.

'Yes, there is something you can do for me.'

'Anything –'

'You can get me permission to visit the hospital. I'm stuck in here because of the edicts and I need some sort of official pass. There are people I need to see at the hospital. You can have a word with whoever is in charge of things like that, if you like.'

He nodded eagerly. 'I will do that,' he promised, and set off. I closed the front door and went back to the table, rubbing my hands. Iris looked up enquiringly.

'I think we've had an answer to the hospital visiting problem,' I said cheerfully, and sat down to our interrupted lunch.

An hour later the Argentine returned. 'Yes, it is approved. You may go to the hospital. I am to escort you. You can take the Monsignor as well.'

I was told I had to carry a white flag, and, not owning such a thing, I made do with a sheet of white foolscap paper. As we walked to St Mary's Presbytery to collect Monsignor Spraggon, the Roman Catholic Prefect Apostolic in charge of St Mary's, we were stopped in the street by an impressive-looking Argentine officer. He exchanged a few brusque words with my escort, and I was introduced.

'This is Padre Bagnall, he is the English minister here.'

The officer looked at me briefly. He seemed a severe, brusque type. 'I am Major Dowling,' he said tersely. He turned to my escort. 'I want you,' he ordered, and exchanged a few sharp sentences of Spanish with him. My guide made his apologies to me and departed on whatever errand Dowling had given him. The Major glanced back at me, inclined his head almost imperceptibly in a nod of dismissal, and began walking briskly away.

'Excuse me, Major—' I said. Dowling raised his eyebrows. I spread my hands. 'I was being escorted by him to the hospital where I have duties with the patients. Do I have your permission to continue?'

Dowling nodded. 'Do not forget to carry your white flag.'

I went off to find Monsignor Spraggon.

It was a strange feeling to be talking to a senior officer of the army that had just invaded my home. I wondered how I should relate to him. Governor Rex Hunt refused to shake hands with the Argentines, insisting that he didn't shake hands with people who came by force. For him that was absolutely right; he is the Queen's representative on the Islands, and it was unthinkable that he should in any way indicate acceptance or approval of the actions of the Argentine army. I believed that for me, it was a different situation. I was a minister of the gospel, and it was my duty to be open to all men without respect to creed or nation. And I am fairly sure that in greeting the Argentine Major in a courteous way I did not give any impression that I was endorsing the actions of his government, any more than Dick Baker and the white flag party did when they allowed Gilobert to effect the usual introductions while negotiating the cease-fire. But Rex Hunt has a different role in this story; the implications of his official position are enormous, and that is why the Argentines treated him as they did.

At the Presbytery I found that the Monsignor was not able to come, and so I collected his colleague Father Monoghan instead. He improvised a white flag for himself out of a linen bag, and together we walked to the hospital clutching our makeshift badges of truce. We passed several groups of armed men and armoured vehicles in Ross Road, but we were not stopped again. We wondered what they made of the two of us – I was dressed in a grey suit and a grey shirt, and he was dressed entirely in clerical black. Some of the soldiers looked rather perplexed at the sight of such an odd couple, one all in grey and the other all in black, and we found ourselves laughing a lot as we picked our way along the street. We reached the hospital shortly after two o'clock.

The hospital, a single-storey brick building with a wooden annexe, is at the end of Ross Road, and is only 150 yards or so from Government House. It was an odd feeling to be so near to the focal point of the morning's fighting, and to know that inside, it was no longer Rex Hunt who was the person in charge of the Island's affairs.

The atmosphere in the hospital was very tense. There were not many people in at the time; most of them were long-stay patients, chiefly elderly people. Father Monoghan and I went round each of them, comforting them and talking with them. They were extremely distressed, and afraid. Some were in tears, others sat hunched up in bed staring bleakly ahead. Most of the fighting and firing had been very near to them, and considering that they had witnessed high-explosive artillery, machine gun fire and flashes and explosions of all kinds, it was remarkable that they were as composed as we found them. Our ministry to them was a matter of taking hold of them and caressing them physically and verbally, giving them some strength and encouragement. There were about six or seven patients in all. We prayed with individuals who asked for prayer, and we stayed for about an hour before leaving. We also took the opportunity to speak to the staff, and our news of what was going on outside was eagerly received.

I walked back with Father Monoghan. We heard on the way that the captured Marines were being held at Government House. I immediately decided that I was going to visit them. My relationship with the Marines as a Royal Navy officiating chaplain was a good one. I spent an hour or so with them every week at their barracks at Moody Brook, and had sometimes been invited to join on some of their activities. They had been good friends of the Cathedral, too – some of our projects had benefited from their help. I had contact with them on military parades, and when I travelled on the MV Forrest on my way to make pastoral visits around the Islands, we had entertained many of them in our home. Now they were being held in detention after a heroic defence of the Islands, and I wanted to spend some time with them.

Before I had worked out how this was to be achieved, I met my Argentine friend again. He was pleased that we had been able to go to the hospital. I made the most of the opportunity to use him again.

'I have heard that the Royal Marines are being held prisoner,' I told him. 'I am the Chaplain of the Marines, and I wish to go to see them. Can you arrange this also?'

Once again permission was given for us to proceed, though we were passed from officer to officer in search of somebody who was prepared to give us the necessary authorisation. Eventually we found a Major who was in charge, and he took us to where the Marines were being held. The weather was very mild, and they were lounging in the sunshine on the grass, in a paddock in front of Government House. They were surrounded by armed guards, and were waiting to find out what was going to happen next. I was able to move among them freely; first I was allowed to speak to the two senior officers, and then to the others. Some of them were well known to me, others had been in the Islands less than a week, and I hadn't yet made contact with them. They told me that six Marines were still uncaptured and that as far as they knew there had been no British casualties. We had already heard over the radio that there were Argentine casualties. I took a number of messages and promised to run several little errands for the Marines. As we talked the guards watched us closely, their guns pointed ready for use if necessary. Afterwards I made my way back to the Deanery. On the way I met one of the residents of the Upland Goose, who invited me to have a cup of tea with him.

The hotel staff were frantically busy—the new authorities had requisitioned all the available beds, and there was a flurry of preparation going on. As we were drinking our tea, at about five o'clock, news came through to the hotel that the Governor was at the broadcasting station on his way to the airport. It was only a matter of a minute and a half's walk from the Deanery to the broadcasting station, so I went there. By this time I had forgotten about the prohibition—I was moving about without being accosted by the soldiers.

When I arrived, His Excellency and his family were getting into the official car, the London taxi flying the official pennant on its bonnet which was a familiar sight in Port Stanley. The Governor had dressed for the occasion in full ceremonial uniform, including the plumed hat of his office. He was criticised for doing so later by various people, mainly outside the Islands, who saw it as unnecessary provocation in an already tense political situation. That is as may be, but it is a great deal easier to analyse these things from the comfort of a critical armchair; being there is a different matter. For many of us at the time, it seemed entirely appropriate that the Governor's role should be emphasised as clearly as possible. If he had worn his full dress uniform simply out of bravado, as a gesture of defiance against the invaders, it would have been understandable; the defence of Government House by the outnumbered British troops had been a display of astonishing bravery, and the Governor had every reason to march out with his head held high. But it was much more than that. It was a reminder to the Argentines that what they were doing was to expel not merely Rex Hunt the colonial civil servant. They were throwing the government out as well.

There were several other families of government officers there as well who were also being put out of the Islands immediately. I took the opportunity to comfort them and say goodbye to them. Quite apart from the emotional significance of what was happening – the Queen's representative being thrown out of the country he served – there were very real fears as well; one of the families was the wife and children of a government servant who had gone to Argentina the week before, so she was understandably upset.

It was therefore quite a tearful occasion. The Governor (whose medals had been ripped off his uniform by an Argentine soldier) was firm and dignified, though you could tell he was bitterly outraged at what was happening – as indeed had been clear from the various broadcasts he had been making through the night and the morning.

There weren't many bystanders – after all, we were supposed to be housebound – but the other clergy were there as well to say goodbye. We made our farewells undisturbed. There were a few Argentine soldiers standing by, mainly to drive the escorting vehicles and the cars in which the other families were riding; but it didn't seem to matter. There were some photographers there as well, mainly Argentine, taking photographs of the whole thing.

The procession moved off. We watched as the cars disappeared along the road towards the Airport. We later heard that they were given a bad time before the plane left, carrying the families who were leaving and the captured Marines. The official flag was confiscated from the bonnet of the taxi, the baggage was searched (several Falkland Island flags which the Governor's son Tony was carrying in his cases were confiscated as well); and all clothing was searched item by item. Having made his point, Rex Hunt changed from his uniform into clothing more suitable for travelling. The official edict had said that the Governor and his family were to be out of the country by four o'clock. In fact it was a little after six o'clock when the plane finally lifted off from Stanley. The Governor had gone. A strict curfew was shortly due to come into operation, so I turned back for home, along streets which bore the scars of the invasion; the iron teeth of the caterpillar tracks had chewed the kerbstones, and there were bullet scars on some of the buildings.

Back at home in the Deanery, Iris and I had a cup of tea and I told her everything that had happened. Looking back on the events of the day, we realised how firmly God had his hand on the situation. I had moved freely about the streets, and had seen all the people I needed to see. I had not felt myself to be in any danger, and the Lord had given me exactly the strength I had needed to get on with the work that needed doing in these new and confusing circumstances. I knew, too, that there would be many people in England and elsewhere praying for us. Our prayer-partners, those who received our newsletters and read of our activities in Intercon's magazine, prayed for us regularly; now I knew that their prayers would be increased as news of events in the Falklands reached them. On that first day of the occupation, as on many days, Iris and I experienced the uplifting power of other people's prayers on our behalf.

We discussed what might happen in the future. Would the British send troops? We didn't know. The silence from London was worrying.

A year before, we had invested several pounds in the purchase of an English-Spanish dictionary, because we had been learning Spanish for two years. We thought then that it might be useful. Some of the Islanders spoke Spanish as well as English, there were Spanish radio broadcasts from South America, and it would be necessary to speak the language when we visited the mainland. Now, as we talked about the future, Iris reminded me. 'We'd better get the language course out,' she said. 'We might need to polish up our Spanish, if this goes on for any length of time.'

She wasn't trying to be funny. Leaving was a real possibility. Already some who had only come to the Islands on a short-term basis were making plans to go; Government officials were being forced to leave; as a clergyman, it would almost certainly have been possible to arrange a speedy departure for Iris and me. But it wasn't an option we consodered. We knew one thing for certain. We were convinced of it, we didn't need to discuss it. We had come to the Islands to do a job, and that job remained to be done; we had come to share the gospel of Jesus Christ. We must stay to do just that.

3: Halfway round the world from Yorkshire

> The Englishman (now, this embraces
> English-speaking people throughout the
> world) still travels or lives abroad for short
> or long periods. His need of the gospel
> remains urgent ... if we say they must
> fend for themselves we fail in our
> Christian duty to care.
>
> *Brian Underwood, 'Faith at the frontiers:*
> *150 years of the Commonwealth and*
> *Continental Church Society'*
> *[Intercontinental Church Society], 1974.*

How does a Yorkshireman in his forties come to be an Anglican minister in a group of islands inhabited by more sheep than people, at the other end of the world?

In my case it was because I knew how to cut up sheep. The advertisement in the *Church Times*, sandwiched in with other notices and easily passed over if you read in a hurry, amused me at first. I smiled as I showed it to my wife. 'Look at this, Iris!'

She read it carefully.

We are looking for an exceptional, adventurous man, married, for the Falkland Islands. Must be physically fit, able to drive and 'de-bog' a Land-rover; butcher own beef and mutton, keep vegetable garden, ducks and hens; dig, dry and burn peat.

She read it again, and gave the paper back to me. 'Harry,' she said thoughtfully, 'Perhaps it's you they're looking for.'

She had a point. The advertisement, placed by the Intercontinental Church Society – (Who? I wondered) – described me exactly. Which was strange, because I would have thought it almost impossible to write an advertisement that so accurately described my odd bundle of experience. There weren't many Church of England clergymen, I reckoned, who had experience in the wholesale butchery trade. But I had.

I was born in Fitzwilliam, a tiny Yorkshire village that boasted at least one claim to fame; the cricketer Geoff Boycott was also born there. When I was five the family moved to Grimethorpe where I first went to school. I finished my education at a Barnsley school and on leaving school became a police cadet. When I was eighteen I received my call-up papers, and entered the army. While I was a soldier I contracted tuberculosis, and that put me on my back for about three years in two long stretches of serious illness. It wasn't until 1953 that I was free from hospital. It was the year of the Coronation, the year of the climbing of Everest – a year of new starts. For me, too.

I'd always been a churchgoer, right from my child-hood when I was sent to Sunday school, more often than not protesting strongly. But my parents were firm, and I went Sunday by Sunday, and that laid the foundations for a knowledge of the Bible and Christianity. When I was twelve I drifted away for two years, but came back because I was interested in singing. From that time onwards I was regularly at church.

But being a Christian, of course, isn't a matter of regular church attendance, it's a matter of how you relate to Jesus Christ. The whole thing became clear to me when I left hospital for the last time, and a growing awareness gripped me that I had been saved – physically saved, from death itself – and that there must be a reason. The local church had been praying for me throughout the time of my illness, and I knew very well that my recovery had been affected by that, and that God had used those prayers in my healing. I had felt carried by those prayers, knowing that people were asking God to heal me, to save my life. But for what? What was it that lay ahead? I didn't know, but I was sure that God had a purpose for my life and had kept me alive because that purpose had to be carried out. That was the time that I gave my life to him, and committed myself to finding out his plan for me and following it. Looking back now, I know that the next few years were really a time of preparation and training, though if anybody had told me at the time, I'd have found it hard to believe. I was convinced that something very special had happened in 1953, though I didn't really understand it until much later.

I went into the meat trade. At that time rationing was still in force, and I worked on the administrative side of the trade until meat was de-rationed a few months later. The Government organisation of which I had been a part broke up and the pre-war structure of the trade re-asserted itself as firms that had been in business before the War started up again. I was asked to join one of these firms, which I did. I became a clerk-salesman.

After a year or so at this I was offered a post as

manager in another town, where I stayed for two years until becoming manager of the Co-operative Wholesale Society's meat department in Sheffield. I was there for five yers, and then worked two years with an Australian frozen meat firm. It was while I was working there that a friend, the Rev. (later Canon) W. Hudson, who had been keeping an eye on me, approached me one day.

'Have you ever thought about doing Christian work?' I considered the idea briefly and shook my head. 'I think I've got all I can handle on my plate at the moment. This job . . .'

'This would be full-time. You'd have to leave the meat business.'

Why not? was my immediate reaction. I'd never thought about my work as something that would continue unchanged until retirement.

'Well,' I said cautiously, 'if you think I've got anything to offer, then – yes, I'm interested. What do you have in mind?'

'It's the Church Missionary Society,' he replied. I knew the Society well; Iris and I had been involved with it for a few years.

I followed the suggestion up. Eventually I was offered a post in the Society's headquarters, with the imposing title of Deputations Secretary – which meant that I ordered other people's lives, sending them around the country to speak at various churches and meetings of all kinds. The people whose lives I organised in this way were returning missionaries, bishops, and so on.

During my time with Society I investigated the possibility of entering the Ministry. There were many influences pointing me in that direction. One was a friend who worked at CMS – the late Harvey Cantrell

–who had visited me ten years before while I was in hospital. Talking to me one day, he looked at me thoughtfully.

'You know, Harry,' he remarked, 'if I had the experience you've got behind you, I think what I'd do is become a hospital chaplain.'

I grinned and shook my head. I wasn't the clergyman type. Far from it; in fact I was the sort of chap who gave the clergy as good as they got, an outspoken layman, the sort of fellow who kept the clergy on their toes. I dismissed the idea.

But the idea took root. At the time we were living in Kent, and attending a church in Murston, where we lived. After the service, people often came back to our home for a cup of coffee and a chat. We enjoyed it, it was a way of sharing our home, and it was exciting to see our lounge packed on a Sunday with people sharing what God had done for them. But what we were finding even more exciting – and thought-provoking – was that many of those people came back as individuals on other days, wanting to talk about their problems and difficulties. It seemed that God had given us a ministry to others in this way. The idea began to appear in the back of our minds that perhaps I ought to look into the possibility of full-time ministry.

Iris encouraged me in scores of ways. We laughed sometimes, when we talked about it, because when she was single she had turned down two proposals of marriage from clergymen. Now it seemed as though she might end up as a clergyman's wife after all.

One tentative step we took, though it didn't lead to anything in job terms, was that I applied to go overseas on Christian work as a layman. My application was turned down on health grounds. I had a significant conversation at the time with Canon H. A. Wittenbach, a friend who had been counselling me about the application.

'One thing they said to me,' I pointed out, 'was that I ought to consider ordination. What do you think?'

He nodded. 'That's an excellent idea. I think you should.'

'Will you support me if I apply to train for the Ministry?' It wasn't an idle request for moral support. He was the sort of person who would only put his name to something he really believed in.

'Of course I will,' he said. It was another sign, an indication we were on the right track.

I went to a CACTM conference. 'CACTM' stood for 'Central Advisory Committee for Training for the Ministry', and the purpose of the weekend conference was to provide a method of assessing applicants for ordination courses. I had several interviews with clerical and lay assessors, and felt that after the weekend was over they had certainly looked into my application very thoroughly. The verdict was not long in coming. My application to go forward for theological training was accepted, but I was recommended for part-time rather than full-time training.

So I joined the Southwark Ordination Course. It was hard work for both of us. The burden of housework and other domestic responsibilities fell on Iris as I grappled with two evening lectures a week and weekends usually taken up by producing written work. One of our precious weekends out of every month was lost because I was away on the course; and the two weeks which previously had been our annual holiday now saw me on residential courses, alone. We had two children by that time, and they were two and five years old; they saw very little of me during those years, and Iris had the task of looking after them almost single-handed. I left home at about 6.30 a.m. to travel to London, and wasn't back until 10 or sometimes 11 at night. So the children didn't see me during the week, and at the weekend, if I was at home, I would be so busy that they would only see me on Sunday. It was a real sacrifice for the family, and especially for Iris; it tested her support for me to the limits. On top of all that – as though that were not enough – she had the task of encouraging me when things got on top of me and I needed cheering up.

I didn't find studying particularly easy. I'm a disciplined sort of person by nature, and I stuck at it, and I managed to get the work done; but I wouldn't say that I was a natural student by any means. However, I satisfied the examiners in due course, did what was required of me, and in 1967 was ordained in the Cathedral of my home diocese, Sheffield.

For the five years after my ordination I served curacies in Goole and Doncaster, and then was given my own church, St Hugh, Cantley, Doncaster. And while in Doncaster, in my first parish, I opened the *Church Times* one day and read the advertisement appealing for a clergyman with butchering expertise.

We'd been in the parish for seven and a half years. We were very happy there; there was no reason to move. I only looked at the advertisements and announcements in the *Church Times* to keep track of the movements of my friends in the ministry. But it wasn't long before an application to the Intercontinental Church Society was dispatched, and we waited to see what would happen. In the meantime we found out what we could about the Society. We discovered that it was a long-established missionary society which existed to place chaplains in areas where there was a need to serve expatriates and English-speaking communities abroad. The Falkland Islands was one of those areas, and the job advertised was the first chaplaincy that the ICS had established in the Islands, though there had been previous Anglican incumbents – the Falkland Islands with their lovely Cathedral had once been a vast diocese which included almost the whole of South America. Now in 1979 the Falkland Islands stood on their own in the Anglican communion as a special area, whose clergyman was directly answerable to the Archbishop of Canterbury (to whom the successful applicant would be similarly directly responsible).

We received a fuller job description from the Society within a few days. While it wasn't as punchy and amusing as the advertisement, the more extended details of what the job involved made us more and more interested. Iris had some doubts when she saw the full job description as to whether I would be eligible for the post – 'A bit too old and not fit enough!' was her first thought – it sounded a really demanding task. But we continued with our application and were called for an interview.

We were interviewed at the Society's headquarters in London, and immediately, even before the job was offered to us, we felt a part of that family. Right from the start we felt sure that this was the next step for us. Difficulties arose, as they always do, but they were removed in miraculous ways. We made preparations and began to say our goodbyes to family and friends. We did not know how long we would be living in the Falklands. All we knew was that in three years' time we would be home on furlough.

At 7.30 in the evening of 8 October 1979, we said goodbye at Heathrow Airport to a group of well-wishers from Intercon, and boarded our plane. Twenty hours later, weary and jet-lagged, we arrived at Buenos Aires. Here we stayed with the Bishop and his wife overnight before boarding a second, slower plane for Commodoro. There we stayed overnight at a hotel where nobody spoke English. After breakfast the next day we began the three-hour flight to Port Stanley.

Our long journey from London had been tedious; we had seen little from the plane, and the airports we stopped at were all in darkness. The local plane was different. We flew over scores of islands, patches of bleak, barren rock dotted in the blue morning sparkle of the sea. We began to feel excited for the first time, and it really seemed possible that we were on the other side of the world from Doncaster. Finally we began the descent into Stanley airport, and the plane touched down on the strip of ground which two years later was to be the focus of the world's attention for ten weeks, but which for us then was simply the last step on our long journey to a new life.

4: The Falkland Islands

At the end of January we took the Rover
to drive over what is called North Camp.
We had 5 days visiting 4 settlements or
farms as well as a mad chase to a beauty
spot to see King Penguins . . .

Letter to prayer-partners, February 1981.

Today, of course, everyone knows what the Falkland
Islands look like. News photographs, television cover-
age and several books written by journalists who
covered the War have ensured that the image of our
sparse, virtually treeless homeland is fixed firmly in
the popular imagination. In Port Stanley, there are
streets and buildings which have been much photo-
graphed; and Government House itself has been the
subject of a good many military maps, showing exactly how the Marines managed their remarkable
defence of the building. It makes no difference that a
copse is misplaced in one representation, that the
main drive of Government House in another map is
drawn on the wrong side of the building. By and
large, the world knows what the Falkland Islands and
their capital look like. And that's not a bad thing.

But for Iris and myself, stepping on to Falklands soil for the first time, it was all quite new. The reading and studying we'd done before we came, since receiving the news from the Intercontinental Church Society that our application had been successful, hadn't prepared us for the reality of this remote place. Even the tedium of the journey was unexpected, a sharp reminder of just how far we had come and how difficult it was to get here.

There are so many things that photographs cannot show. You can do your homework, look at pictures, see films and talk to people, but when you are actually standing in the place you've spent so much time studying, it differs from your expectations in scores of unexpected ways.

Nothing had prepared us, for example, for the extraordinary windiness of the Island. The Falklands climate is an odd phenomenon: there can be bright, sunny days, when the sun bakes down through the crystal clear air (no pollution here from factories and furnaces). On days like that, an unwary visitor is easily tricked by the warmth of the sun into removing cardigans or shirts, only to find that the gentle breeze which had seemed insignificant was in fact disguising just how hot the sun actually was. It may seem strange to see sunburn and peeling skin less than 500 miles from Cape Horn, but it is not by any means unknown. The local people are not easily fooled by the weather. We are used to having Summer, Autumn, Winter and Spring following each other in the space of a single day – sometimes even a single hour – and it's rare to find anybody who lives in the Falklands sunbathing.

You cannot prepare yourself, either, for the strangeness of finding that this isolated group of islands is distinctly British in atmosphere. This bleak, windy place was uninhabited until the first British settlers arrived here. English is the only language, and almost all the inhabitants are British. 'Like liberating a suburban golf-club,' was the comment of one British journalist after the relief of Port Stanley in June 1982. He had a point. As we rode into Stanley that morning we saw bright red British post-boxes, trim pavements and kids playing around on bikes in the road like kids in Doncaster which we had left 8,000 miles behind us.

But we were aware of other things too – only dimly, but enough to remind us that we really were in a distant country. The rough hills and scrub behind the town were unlike anything we had seen in Britain; the houses were built mainly of wood, and there were few trees worth speaking of in the gardens of the town; and over everything, despite the gusting wind, lay the sweet-earth smell of peat fires. Later, as we came into Ross Road and along the harbour wall, we saw derelict hulks lying at crazy angles against equally derelict jetties; the hulks were the relics, we were to find later, of unsuccessful attempts to round the Horn in bitter weather.

We were greeted at the Airport by a welcoming party; the Church secretary and one of the Church wardens, and one or two others. Our luggage was gathered together and we were shown to a Landrover, in which we made the bumpy journey into Port Stanley. We saw the multi-coloured houses of the town, and among them the larger public buildings including the Cathedral with its prominent tower, which was to be the focus of my work. This was the beautiful building I'd read about, once the focus of a huge diocese, now the Anglican Church of the Falkland Islands; when it was built, it was intended as a refuge for sailors, a Parish Church for the Islands, and the Cathedral Church for most of a continent. It is no longer the Cathredal for that Diocese, but we see a good many sailors there (I am Chaplain to the Missions to Seamen), and it *is* the Parish Church. So two out of three of the founders' aims are still intact. The Cathedral stands on Ross Road, at the edge of the harbour, just a few minutes from my home.

We were warmly welcomed by our new neighbours. Another Church warden was our hostess for lunch that first day, and when we were finally installed in the Deanery, a succession of callers brought us gifts of eggs, cakes and vegetables. It was a first taste of the good home-grown food we enjoy in Stanley, and the kindness and generosity of the people. Before very long we had begun our own gardening. Although it's very pleasant in England to get out into the garden and grow one's own food, on the Falkland Islands it is a necessity. Vegetables are not always available, and can be expensive when they are. We soon learned the importance of a well-stocked freezer.

We had many new experiences to come to terms with and many skills to learn. Iris had to learn the techniques of a peat-fired Rayburn oven; I had to acquaint myself with the mechanics of getting peat, a process which starts with the digging (though the peat is free, the costs of cutting and transport can be quite high), and culminates in the tossing-and-turning drying process known as 'rickling'.

Out on the peat common, wielding the special peat-spade (it has a hole drilled in the blade so that the suction of the soggy peat can easily be broken), one feels more than anywhere else the isolation and beauty of the Islands. Away from the township with its echoes of England, up on the hills with the wind whipping at one's clothing, it is not easy to forget that this is one of the world's remote and lonely places. What vegetation there is on the island is sparse. The rough tufty grass of the moorlands, deceptively firm-looking but in reality often concealing standing water in which the unwary walker can easily find himself sinking knee-deep, gives way to the wide expanses of peat-bog, crumbling and dry in warm weather and treacherously wet after rain. Essential items of equipment to carry in the Landrover are a spade and a bumper jack, because on a trip across the camp it is likely that the vehicle will be bogged down more than once. The *Church Times* advertisement was strictly practical when it listed de-bogging Landrovers as part of my job specification!

Wild flowers are not numerous. Only a few hardy varieties are to be found, tucked into the shelter of scrub or scree, or in the clefts of the 'stone runs' (literally, rivers of quartzite rocks formed by geological processes). The teaberry, which has many uses in cooking, is difficult to find, but worth the hunt; the fruit has a sweet flavour with a hint of nutmeg. The diddle-dee is almost the national plant of the Falklands, and has even found its way into the Islands' language; to hear something by 'diddle-dee telegraph' is to hear it by a mysterious and extremely fast word-of-mouth, and the system was almost over-worked during the invasion.

There is a great variety of animal and bird life. Of course there are the ubiquitous sheep, on which the economy of the Islands depends and without which there would be little point in anyone living in the Falklands at all. There are all domestic animals except the goat. Wild creatures abound, including the famous upland geese, after which the Hotel next door to the Deanery is named, and penguins, seals, and a diversity of seabirds. All the land mammals on the Islands have been brought from outside.

The people among whom we had come to live and work are not numerous. A census in 1980 indicated that the population was 1,813; of these, 1,360 were born in the Islands and therefore were entitled to the name of 'Kelpers', which comes from the seaweed that surrounds much of the coast. It is a proud title to bear in the Islands, and as in most isolated rural communities, newcomers have to earn acceptance, which is cautiously given. But once accepted into the community, the immigrant Falkland Islander will find, as we have found, that the people are warm-hearted, friendly, and extremely generous with their hospitality. Most of the inhabitants of the Islands make their living from the sheep-farming industry. The two main employers in the Islands are the Local Government with its various service departments such as Public Works and Education; and the Falkland Islands Trading Company. Social life and recreation is varied—there are several very good craft workers, and spinning, weaving and knitting are all popular. There are dances both in Port Stanley and at various farms; there is a football ground in Port Stanley, and two annual sports weeks, one for East Falkland and one for West Falkland. Horse-racing, steer-riding and other less hectic sports are all well-attended. Sports are all well-supported. Similar events are held in Port Stanley on Boxing Day and the following day.

But against this it has to be remembered that peat-cutting and gardening take up the majority of most people's time and that left for sports and recreation is limited.

About half of the people live in Port Stanley, the only town on the Islands; the rest live in the forty or so outlying farms and settlements. To properly understand what it was like to be in Stanley during the invasion, you have to constantly bear in mind that the town has normally a population of 900 people. It is quite possible to walk from one end of Stanley to the other in a matter of minutes. It sits in the shadow of Mount London, Tumbledown and Sapper Hill, which form a three-sided cradle. The fourth aspect of the town is of course the harbour, a long inlet into the coast which forms the splendid natural shelter for ships which made the town's founders decide to build in that particular place. But forget images of large thriving docks and harbour buildings. Stanley is a small town, and the simple port services available are adequate for the needs of the people it serves.

In Stanley there are three churches – the Anglican Cathedral, the Roman Catholic Church of St Mary, and the non-conformist Tabernacle Church. The official census figures for the Islands showed Anglicans as the largest group (900 plus), Nonconformists as numbering 300, Roman Catholics as numbering 210, and about 200 Ba'hai, Jehovah's Witnesses, and undenominational Christians. 107 inhabitants said that they had no religious beliefs. Of course census figures are a risky way of assessing the relative true state of affairs in such matters as church attendance, and a reasonable practical estimate for Cathedral attendance would be that about ten per cent of the population of Stanley attend the Cathedral regularly. My relationship with the other churches in Port Stanley is a friendly one. I live near the Roman Catholic presbytery and enjoy the friendship of Monsignor Spraggon and Father Monoghan, and I have been required from time to time to take funeral services at the free church Tabernacle, which is at the time of writing without a full-time minister. Oddly enough, it is the Roman Catholic Church which is known locally as the 'Chapel'.

Even before the events of April 1982, the Falkland Islanders were always avowedly British, and this shows itself in many ways – there are numerous reminders of Britain in the people's homes and in the streets and public places. The Governor of the Islands has a special place in the community because he is the Queen's representative. I came to the Falklands towards the end of Governor Parker's term of office, and was therefore present at the public swearing-in of Rex Hunt, his successor. He is a genial, approachable man respected as much for his own personality as for the office he holds, and he takes an active interest in every aspect of Island life. When I first met him, at a Town Hall reception after the swearing-in, he shook hands briskly.

'You're at the Cathedral?'

I nodded.

'Well, I look forward to seeing you there on Sunday,' he remarked, 'and I shall be there whenever I am in Port Stanley on a Sunday.'

He has been as good as his word. Also I think it is true to say that he has visited every farm on the Islands, some more than once, and when round-the-world travellers berth their yachts at Port Stanley they are usually invited to visit him at Government House during their stay. He makes his home available to organisations helping elderly people, and he and his wife adopt an 'open door' policy towards anybody who wants to go and talk to him about any matter in which they need his help. He is a symbol of British government, and a much-liked person in his own right.

Our work in the Islands involves a great deal of travelling; often it means that we are away from Port Stanley for several days at a time. We travel by Landrover (a gift to the Church from the Bradford Diocese) or by plane, or by boat. When we arrived in the Islands the Falkland Islands Government Air Service had three planes, two beaver float planes and one Islander Aircraft. Also there were in 1979 two privately-owned Cesna light aircraft. The rather pioneering spirit that one acquires as a passenger in these small craft is enhanced by the fact that the telephone service is restricted to Port Stanley, and cross-Island communication is normally by 2-metre radio or 'RT' (radio telephone).

Ministering to those living in 'Camp' (the Falklands name, borrowed from South America, for the rural hinterland) is quite unlike any other ministry I have ever known. If it is difficult for us to get to them, it is equally difficult for them to get to us. The families in Camp may visit Port Stanley once a year or even less frequently. When we go to these outlying farms and settlements, it is our once-a-year visit to them. This means that our times of fellowship are times of reunion as well, and we try to provide as much help as we can for the time before our next visit. Iris is in charge of our literature work. When we arrived in the Islands we found that there was no place from which one could buy a Bible, and Christian books and magazines were virtually unobtainable. We imported a stock of Bibles and other material and made them available for the people of Stanley and those living in the Camp. We don't make any profit on this, and we were able to make arrangements with some of the stores to have books from us. The storekeepers have been very helpful – they themselves resell at cost, so there is no profit for them in the transactions either. We distribute a great deal of Christian literature, including books of general interest, evangelistic material, and Bible-reading courses and aids.

We are also often asked to hold special services in the places we visit – in one farm, where a young couple live with their three children, we were asked to baptise the youngest child; we showed a Church Pastoral Aid Society film strip on baptism to a congregation which consisted of the family, the farm-workers and a farm manager who chanced to be in the area (the projector is one designed to work from our car battery). Then the service of baptism was held before we left, attended by that small congregation.

We have Holy Communion in some of the places we visit, often sitting round a farmhouse kitchen table. Our services of worship are attended by farm workers and others living in the locality. We are the guests of the farm managers. The courtesy and generosity extended to us by these men and their wives is very much appreciated, as is the warmth of the welcome that we receive from the tenants themselves.

Iris has a special ministry to the children, and makes good use of a number of teaching aids. 'Link and Learn' is a joint venture organised by Scripture Union and Intercon. It provides Bible stories and lessons intended for children who are living in isolated situations. 'Link and Learn' materials are sent to Iris each month, and she has over a dozen children in different parts of the Islands who recieve them. For most of these children, this is the only form of Bible study available to them, as Sunday School is out of the

59

question in the scattered farms. The children enjoy the scheme very much. Parents often join in and help the children to work through the month's notes, and when Iris visits their home she spends time with the children, discussing what they have learned.

Children in the 'Link and Learn' scheme are eligible to join the Walt Club, named from the initial letters of its motto, 'We all learn together.' A club newsheet is distributed from London, and children are encouraged to write to Scripture Union with their news and greetings. Several children in the Falkland Islands have written to the Walt Club and sent pictures of their homes and the animals on their farms.

Scripture Union's *Quest Notes* for children are also popular, and recently Iris formed a 'Quest Club', based on Bible reading competitions and other activities. Materials to do with this, and a good supply of other Bible reading helps, are always left with families that have children.

In Port Stanley, of course, the Cathedral is the focus of our work. The Sunday services we offered in the Cathedral were the eight o'clock Holy Communion; the ten o'clock Family Communion, at which the Sunday School children were present and, after the opening hymn, the little ones were taken through to the Church Hall for teaching; then in the evening we had the seven o'clock Evensong, broadcast on alternate Sundays for the benefit of the housebound and those living in Camp. On Wednesday and Thursday we held Communion services, and on Thursday evening at eight o'clock there was a Bible study in the Deanery in which we studied the lesson for the next Sunday.

Part of my duties as Chaplain mean that I am required to attend the opening of the Island's Legislative Council (which happens once or twice a year) and say prayers. Originally the clergyman in the Falklands was a colonial Chaplain, and I think that my presence in the opening of the Council is a continuance of the tradition, though I am not a colonial Chaplain (another legacy of that tradition is that a part of the incumbent's stipend is paid by the Government).

This then was the pattern of our work in the Islands before the events of April 1982: a combination of pastoral work in a remote setting, and the weekly and daily routines of a parish church which also happened to be a Cathedral. When the Argentines arrived, and the structure of our life as Falkland Islanders changed, one big question hung over everything for me as a minister of the gospel. What would change? What freedom would we have? What was in store for the Church of Christ in the Falklands?

5: Occupied

> Whatever the outcome, Iris and I wish to
> stay to carry on with our work.
>
> *Letter to prayer-partners, Easter Day.*

We slept soundly the first night of the invasion – not
surprisingly, considering the crowded events of the
day and the broken night that had preceded it.

Next morning I awoke feeling refreshed. I spent my
usual time before breakfast praying and reading the
Bible. I prayed, talking to the Lord about the people I
proposed to visit that day and bringing before him
others whom I knew were sick or frightened or
elderly. After breakfast, I said goodbye to Iris and left
the house promptly at nine o'clock. My plan was to
move around the houses of the older people whom I
knew, to visit them and see how they were bearing up
under the stress of the invasion. I went on my own,
and had no white flag – I had by then completely forgotten the regulations about being housebound. I had
telephoned a number of people the day before to find
out how they were, and now I had decided on a course
through the streets which took in most of the people I
needed to visit. As I walked I was amazed at the

numbers of soldiers now in the town. They were standing in groups, some just talking, others doing weapons drill or exercising under the eye of a commanding officer.

I went on to the Airport road, on which there are a number of prefabricated houses, quite flimsy constructions: these were the houses which had been in the front line of the shooting the day before, whose occupants we had heard telephoning in to the broadcasting studio to report the latest state of affairs. It was very clear that there had been heavy fighting. Ejected rifle shells and spent ammunition were scattered all over the street, and the road surface bore the scars of the army vehicles. Some of the houses were so badly damaged it was incredible that with such damage, no one had been killed. I met one of the young mothers in the road, and we spent some time talking; then I moved on and began calling at the houses. Here they were mostly young, expatriate people, some extremely shocked by what had happened. They were beginning to discuss what their plan should be – whether they should go back to the UK or stay in Stanley.

One house seemed more badly damaged than the rest. It looked empty as I walked by, but a neighbour in another house told me that the tenant was at home. So I went back to the house. The front doors in Stanley are rarely locked, and it was no different that morning. I knocked and went inside. The resident had been in the Islands years ago, had moved away, and had come back a short time before to enjoy some peace and quiet in Port Stanley. His plans had of course been dramatically frustrated, as he demonstrated by showing me the damage that the house had received. The roof had a gaping hole in it, and a radiator had been literally shredded by the blast. In the bedroom, he and his wife had sheltered under the double mattress because the bed was designed in such a way it wasn't possible to shelter underneath it. The blast had occurred only a few feet away, the other side of a flimsy wall, yet they had both been uninjured. (One of the remarkable things about the invasion, and something for which we gave thanks to the Lord, was that there were no civilian casualties at all; they were at risk, the houses were lightweight and under attack, but no one was harmed.)

We talked together as he mopped up the floor which was soaked with water from the burst radiator, and I also talked to his wife; they were both very cheerful in view of the circumstances.

Talking to an 80-year-old lady later, she described to me how the troops had appeared and moved down the road into the town; it had been a traumatic experience. But she too was very cheerful. 'It could have been a lot worse,' she reminded me, 'a lot worse. And the house isn't damaged.' (Sadly, a few weeks later, she became the third civilian to die in the conflict.)

I left her home and moved on. Soldiers glanced at me curiously but made no move. At intervals, enormous track-laying vehicles trundled past loaded with men and weapons. Armoured vehicles were still being unloaded from landing craft in the harbour and rolling into the town. It appeared that some sort of patrol was in operation, a visible reminder of the enormous armed strength that was now in charge. There was a good deal of bad temper and irritation when Argentine vehicles negotiating our narrow streets took the right hand side, and encountered our local drivers who were coming at them on the 'wrong' side of the road.

My next visit was to the oldest couple in our congregation. The lady was very distressed; I doubt if even now she has completely recovered from the shock of that weekend. They eventually left the Islands and are now living in England. Another family I visited was a couple living with an elderly parent. They were delighted to see me – that morning I was made welcome wherever I went, and it didn't make any difference whether or not the families were members of our congregation. Their situation was similar to the others I had seen; trying to concentrate on the normal daily routine, but evidently very much on edge and jumping at the sound of military action in the street outside. They greeted me warmly, obviously very relieved to see a familiar face. The conversations revolved around the damage done to the various homes, concern about injuries to the population and the fate of Government House, and gratitude that with so much military activity going on, Port Stanley had got off so lightly. There was a general sense of relief, because the worst seemed to be over, they were still alive, their homes were not destroyed, and they were uninjured.

Towards lunchtime I made my way back towards home. I noticed an Argentine army padre wearing an eye-patch; he was some way away, and I did not stop to speak. I had a job to do. Making sure that the soldiers were not taking any notice of what I was doing, I surreptitiously lowered the flagpole that stood in my garden and stowed it away safely. Whatever else happened to the house, I did not want to see the flag of Argentina flying over it.

I shared my news with Iris, who was of course very anxious to know how our neighbours were managing. Many of them were people we prayed for regularly, and we felt a great concern for them, especially the elderly. As I described the morning's visiting to her it crossed my mind that the whole thing had probably been an illegal outing – I suddenly recalled the radio edicts forbidding people to leave their homes. But nobody had challenged me in the streets. Perhaps the clerical collar I was wearing helped. In any case, by lunchtime and life was beginning to return to Port Stanley.

But it was a very strange life that returned. During the day an announcement was made that people could now go about the streets, but identification had to be carried at all times. The curfew was lifted, and the shops opened, and so did the pubs – accompanied by an edict from the new authorities warning that 'provocation and drunkenness' would be dealt with by military patrols. The broadcasting station under its new management returned to a limited service; the BBC News was not allowed, because diplomatic relations between the United Kingdom and Argentina were now severed. However, the sports report was allowed on the air. This was probably a heavy gesture of conciliation to us from the Argentines, who had by then begun their campaign of informing us that it was good to be Argentine and the invasion was the best thing that had ever happened to the Islanders. In fact the effect of all this was quite opposite; as I moved around visiting, I found that the people who had previously been 'middle-of-the-road' in the Falklands-Argentine dispute had mostly become hardline anti-Argentine overnight.

I stayed at home for the rest of the day. I had to think about my sermon for the following evening.

The last verse of the hymn came to an end and there

followed the familiar shuffle of people seating themselves in pews. I entered the pulpit and looked down. It was an unusually large congregation. Habitually people fill the back seats first; only the Governor and his party can be relied on to sit at the front. But I looked down at individuals and families sitting packed in the pews, my friends and neighbours. I saw their faces looking up at me, I could see several handkerchiefs being applied to eyes rather than noses. As I looked at the congregation I had to blink my own tears away. A sense of sadness was evident in the congregation, but also a sense of expectation. And at the back, sitting unobtrusively near the door, was a young Argentine soldier staring at his boots.

It was Palm Sunday, the first Sunday after the invasion. I had prepared a sermon some time in advance, including in it the Governor's visit to Roy Cove which had been planned for April 2nd. On that day he had been due to fly out to the new owners of some land allocations there, and make a formal presentation of the documents of ownership. Of course because of the invasion, that had not happened, and instead of flying to Roy Cove, His Excellency flew out of the country on April 2nd. My Palm Sunday sermon, however, was to have used the presentation, and the enthusiasm of the new owners of their land, as a sermon illustation. Now, that sermon was useless.

So the sermon I preached that Sunday evening was a different sermon. But it wasn't an impromptu one. It was carefully thought out and prayed over. Preaching it was for me a tense experience, because I had to keep my emotions in check. I was preaching to people who were distressed, a condition I shared with them. Also, the Cathedral services are broadcast on alternate Sundays to the rest of the Islands, and as this was one of those Sundays the Argentines permitted the broadcast to go ahead.

I preached from Jeremiah chapter 29 and Matthew chapter 22, which were the lessons for that Sunday. I intended to give a message of hope, but I wanted also to bring a message of not miserably sitting down, but of making the best of it, getting on with the job. Look at Jeremiah's message to his people, I said: in exile, what were they to do? To long for the days of yesteryear? Not at all. He told them to settle down, raise their families, build their houses ... 'It is not me giving the advice,' I pointed out. 'It is Jeremiah using God's Word.' And indeed it was a wonderful passage of the Bible to find in the lectionary for that day, one which seemed peculiarly appropriate to our new situation. As I came to the end of the sermon I was preaching to myself as much as to the people sitting in front of me. 'Yes, we are living in dangerous times ... we cannot see what is going to happen. Even so, come on, pick yourself up – don't panic or run away; perhaps for the first time in your life you are going to find out what trusting in God really means.' In what really was the darkest day for the Falkland Islands, the Old Testament seemed to speak with a new and exciting relevance.

Like most other churches we give out miniature palm crosses on Palm Sunday. Because there aren't any palm trees in Port Stanley, we use tussock grass, a strong wiry leaf which is very common on the Islands. The events of the last few days had meant that we had not been able to prepare the crosses as usual. That Sunday morning, after the ten o'clock service, I had been approached by a very distressed and worried young man who was anxious to leave Port Stanley and stay in Camp. I promised to give him a lift, so later that day I drove him several miles out of town and dropped him at the place where he had arranged to be picked up by his friends from one of the settlemnents. On the way back I had an idea. I stopped the Rover by the roadside and tore an armful of diddle-dee from the ground. This was now lying at the back of the church.

'We have no tussock crosses,' I said, 'but there is a pile of diddle-dee by the door. Please take a sprig and wear it as your Palm Sunday cross, as a symbol of our unity.' The idea was taken up by a large number of people, and one or two (including myself) wore our diddle-dee sprigs for the whole period of the invasion.

It was a wonderful service, charged with deep emotion and a strong sense of purpose. At the end, we would normally have sung the National Anthem when the Govenor or his representative were present. Rex Hunt had left the Islands, but his assistant Dick Baker, who was usually acting Governor, was at the service. We had been forbidden by the military authorities to sing the National Anthem, which would have counted as provocation. But instead, at the end, on an impulse I asked he congregation to sing Auld Lang Syne. It was an intensely moving moment, because the service was being broadcast, which made it a moment for the whole of the Island to share.

During the service the young Argentine became quite obviously distressed and tearful. At the end, as I moved to the back of the church, I wondered how other people were going to react to this soldier sitting there. I was pleased to notice that they were all compassionate; they all felt sorry for him. I suppose that, like me, they assumed he was homesick or something like that. When I spoke to him, however, he shook his head. It was the sermon that had disturbed him. 'To think,' he said softly, 'I have travelled as far as this – in order to find my direction in life!'

Later that Sunday I learned that the last of the Marines who had been holding out in Camp, a patrol that had eluded the Argentines and were still at large after the others had been sent home, had surrendered. They were now in detention in Port Stanley, waiting to leave the Islands.

I and Monsignor Spraggon requested permission to visit them, and at seven o'clock that evening we were allowed five minutes with them in their cell. There were six men, five Protestant and one Roman Catholic. I was allowed five minutes with five men in one room, and we successfully stretched the five minutes to ten. It was a good meeting. They were cheerful and uninjured, and their main concern was that their families should be told that they were safe. I promised to do what I could, and when I left I was thinking hard how I could get the information to the families. At that point in the occupation we were allowed to send messages by cable or wireless, providing that the messages were not of a military nature. So I could hardly send a telegram to the Royal Marines HQ detailing the present disposition of their men, and in any case the captured Marines had been prevented by the Argentines from giving me their addresses.

Eventually I hit on a way of getting the information out. A former OC of the Marines was a clergyman's son, and I had been corresponding with his father. Next morning I went to the Cable and Wireless offices and sent him the following telegram: 'Tell Robin's boss, Mike Norman's children all well.' Robin was the clergyman's son, and Mike Norman was the new OC who had arrived with the Marines in the Islands a few days before the invasion.

Later that day I received a telegram in reply: 'Thank you very much, all's well.' I was very glad to know that my little ruse had worked and the news had got through.

The curfew imposed on us meant that we were all in our houses earlier than usual each night. But there was so much to do that the days seemed to me longer than before. The pattern of those first few days became the normal one; visiting, talking to people, comforting them, praying with those who wished to, and making myself useful in any practical ways I could. In the beginning, many people were too shocked and distressed to think. But gradually, as the days passed, there emerged a spirit of passive defiance. It was nothing I could isolate or describe fully. It was more a mood, a desire to live every minute, to laugh whenever possible; not cringing, just getting on with living.

Interlude

Communique Number 4

Guarantees

The Governor of the Islas Malvinas, Georgia del Sur and Sandwich del Sur, General of Division Osvaldo Jorge Garcia, notifies the population that: Faithfully upholding the principals stated in the National Constitution and in accordance with the customs and tradtions of the Argentine people it guarantees:

1st. The continuity of the way of life of the people of the Islands

2nd. Freedom of worship

3rd. Respect for private property

4th. Freedom of labour

5th. Freedom to enter, leave, or remain on the Islands

6th. Improvement of the population's standard of life

7th. Normal supply situation

8th. Health assistance

9th. Normal function of essential public services

Furthermore the population is exhorted to continue

normally with their activities from the moment in which this will be stated with the support of the Argentine government in an atmosphere of peace, order and harmony.

Islas Malvinas April 2nd 1982

Edict 2

The Commander of the Malvinas operation orders the following:

1. Radio amateur transmissions throughout Malvinas territory, South Georgia and South Sandwich Islands are forbidden from April 6th. This prohibition includes all bands and types of transmissions.
2. Any transgression to this edict is an infringement to the law and will be judged by a special court martial . . .
3. Every person who infringes the regulations established by article 1 will be punished with one month to two years imprisonment . . . or be sanctioned with 1 to 6 months of arrest according to the ruling of the court . . . participation or complicity or concealment will be punished according to the code of military justice and the Argentine penal code . . .

Islas Malvinas April 6th 1982

. . . .

I never met General Garcia. We heard his broadcasts shortly after the invasion, but I would not have known who he was if I had met him in the street. He was only

in charge for a short time. On the 7th, General
Menendez arrived to become Military governor. I
consulted Dick Baker, Rex Hunt's assistant, a short
time before Menendez's swearing-in.

'Look here,' I asked him, 'Have you had an invitation to this inauguration do at the Town Hall?'

'I have, yes. Have you?'

'Yes – so have quite a few of us. What d'you think I
should do, Dick?'

He laughed. 'If I were you, Harry, I should do
exactly what you think best.' He winked at me.

That was how I came to miss the swearing-in of the
Argentine military governor.

6: Getting going again

There was considerable humour. We saw
a cartoon with the names of the ships in
our part of the force . . . and below is the
caption, 'The Empire strikes back'. And
one group said they'd already booked a
dance hall for the night they landed in
Port Stanley.

*Brian Hanrahan, BBC correspondent with
the Task Force, April 10.*

The two majors were clearly embarrassed. The large
box at their feet sat prominently on the Deanery steps
as they tried to make light of its presence.

'It is a gift,' said one.

'Yes,' the other emphasised. 'It is a gift, a present
from us to you.'

'A gift for your church, for the people to whom you
minister.' The first major waxed lyrical. His colleague
chimed in.

'Of course, there is no charge. It is a gift.' I looked
at the box without enthusiasm. The name and symbols of a leading Japanese television company were
prominent all over it.

'But I don't want it,' I said. 'Neither do my parishioners.'

They were crestfallen. 'We have begun television transmissions to the Malvinas. You will receive programmes. Entertainment, sport . . .'

'No thank you.' I shook my head. 'We have never had television in the Falkland Islands and we do not want it now.' The majors tactfully ignored my refusal to rechristen the Islands. 'I cannot accept this gift,' I continued. 'It is unwanted and it will not be used.'

The majors' tone became pleading. 'We have no wish to compromise you. We are inaugurating transmissions and we wish to donate this television set to your church. Please accept it. It is a gift.'

Eventually I gave in. 'Very well. I accept your gift. Thank you.'

The majors brought the box into the Deanery with relief, and left with cordial farewells. I called Iris. 'What is it?' she asked as she came into the room.

'It's a television,' I said.

She raised her eyebrows. 'It's a gift,' I explained. 'From the Argentines.'

We contemplated the box together. Then we put it away, unopened, in a corner. It is still unused today.

If the invasion were to be thought of as a 'shotgun wedding', the month of April might aptly be called the honeymoon period. The Argentines put considerable effort into wooing the Islands they had taken by force; the official communiques blunted the edge of the demands they made by much talk of the future benefits that lay in store for us now that we were Argentine residents. The armed forces tried very hard to be popular. Instructions had obviously been issued to ensure that relationships with the Islanders were to be correct and considerate. For myself, I was treated with courtesy and respect. I understand Monsignor Spraggon had contact with some of the more devout soldiers and established workable relationships. Because he was the RC Prefect Apostolic he was accorded considerable respect, and his influence was found very useful when he and I had protests to make to the authorities. On the first Sunday a company of Argentine high-ranking officers and some of their men attended Mass at St Mary's Church. Their presence rather subdued the usual congregation, partly because it was unnerving to find oneself in church with one's conquerors, and partly because the Argentines brought their weapons into the church with them. Their entrance was accompanied by the thumping and scraping of automatic guns being dragged into pews. There was no intention to use them in the church, merely a refusal to leave them outside.

The Argentines continued to consolidate their invasion with a massive military build-up in the Falklands. Britain's response, despite considerable reluctance to actually declare that a state of war existed, was swift. On Monday April 5, the first Task Force ships left Porstmouth after a weekend of frenzied preparation; the following Wednesday, a 200-mile military exclusion zone around the Falklands was declared by Britain, to come into effect from April 12th. The Argentines were not sure how determined the British were to follow through with an attempt to retake the Islands, but were leaving nothing to chance. In the days before the implementation of the Zone, men and arms were flown into Port Stanley at an increasing rate. It was in those days just after the invasion, when travel from the outside world was still unhindered, that a North American journalist interviewed me. I was standing on the Cathedral steps when he walked past. When he saw me he retraced his steps.

'This your church?'

'This is the Cathedral. Yes, it's my church.'

'Mind if I interview you for a minute or two?'

I had no objection, but as the interview proceeded I became worried. The 'minute or two' became fifteen minutes or more. Afterwards I was really concerned about the effect the interview might have; not because I was worried that I could have put myself in personal danger by being outspoken, but that the interview might bring me to the attention of the Argentine authorities and that I might consequently be labelled an undesirable agitator, to be shipped off the Islands at the first opportunity. Nothing could have been further from my wishes. I wanted to stay in the Falklands, ministering to the people to whom God had sent me. The job was still there to be done. I didn't want to be taken away from it. However, after a few days of anxiety (and much prayer) I heard no more about it.

Most of the public buildings in the town were taken over to accommodate the incoming troops. The schools, the Town Hall, the gymnasium and even the Cathedral Hall were marked by the forces as requisitioned. But the courtesies were observed: owners of private buildings were given compensation when their buildings were commandeered; for the Cathedral Hall, I was offered £200 per month, and managed to extract £250; there was no way of preventing the soldiers from taking possession of the building, so I thought I might as well ensure that the Argentines made as substantial a contribution as possible to church funds. At about the same time, the new television service was launched, and television sets were offered to the public at a fairly cheap price with hire-purchase facilities if required.

We were told of grandiose schemes by which the Argentines would bring us into the twentieth century. They talked about building a new Port Stanley — rather, a new 'Puerto Argentina' — on the Islands, so that we would be able to leave the timber houses in which we had lived for so long, and taste the benefits of modern city life in all its splendour. In particular, they talked about high-rise apartments which would be built for us. According to the Argentines, we had no idea what living in a city could be like, and they intended to give us that privilege.

The people of Port Stanley were not at all impressed by this. The immediate reaction from most residents was that we lived the way we did, not because we were deprived or kept in poverty by the British, but because we liked it that way. In any case, the Argentines, perhaps because they were obsessed with the historical question of sovereignty over the Islands, had not studied the history of the Falklands very closely. Port Stanley was chosen carefully by its founders, and it is doubtful whether there is a better site for a town on East Falkland, even were such a project to be undertaken with the wholehearted support of the people. Nobody took the proposal seriously.

But the efforts of the Argentines to be friendly and obliging in no way concealed or compensated for the fact that we were a country under enemy occupation. From being a community with our own lifestyle, getting on with things at a different pace and with different priorities from those of the world of commerce and cities, we had been thrust into a situation of submission. In the early days of the invasion, a succession of edicts were issued, some of which were sharp reminders that we were now under Argentine rule and things were going to be changed. On the first Monday after the invasion an Argentine was appointed as civilian Radio Controller, and a further blow to our sense of British identity was an instruction that from now on, vehicles must be driven on the right-hand side of the road. The next day the Post Office re-opened under Argentine management and all amateur radio communications were prohibited. On Wednesday our informal highways were dignified by white lines painted down the centre (and arrows to indicate on which side and in which direction we were to drive!). Also on this date – April 7 – General Menendez, the new Argentine military Governor, was sworn in.

The edicts continued. Nobody to be allowed outside their houses without a white flag; Port Stanley to be renamed Puerto Argentina; the radio telephone prohibited except for essential community services; all 2-metre radio equipment to be handed in to the military authorities; petrol to be rationed; and so on. We were still in touch with the outside world by letter and cable. I was in correspondence with Lambeth Palace; I had received telegrams from Intercon, Bishop Cutts of the Diocese of Argentina and Eastern South America, ex-Governor Parker (who had preceded Governor Hunt) and of course members of the family. These messages from the outside world meant a great deal to us. We felt the support of many people. Their prayers really did make a difference.

We listened to the BBC World Service, and we heard the news of the 'shuttle diplomacy' between

Britain, the United States and Argentina and the debates at the United Nations. Apparently the Security Council had passed its Resolution 502 demanding an immediate cessation of hostilities, an immediate Argentine withdrawal, and a return to the negotiating table. The Foreign Secretary, Lord Carrington, had resigned. Francis Pym had taken over. General Alexander Haig, the United States Secretary of State, had begun negotiations between London and Buenos Aires. It was believed that, despite its strong links with Latin America and its concern for the political balance in South America, the United States government would eventually take Britain's side.

It was hard to work up any enthusiasm. Negotiations were always going on about the Falklands; there were negotiations in progress when the invasion took place. How could a new phase of negotiations achieve any more than previous attempts had? The Argentines were here now, in Port Stanley, supported by a massive military strength. What good could talking do now?

We heard also the first announcements, only days after the invasion, of the preparation of the Task Force. At first we found it difficult to believe. Many of the Islanders thought it was merely a face-saving threat, a show of strength without a real commitment to set sail. But as we heard the cheers from the quaysides in England as the first warships set off, there was rejoicing in Port Stanley too.

Morale in the Islands was very much up and down in those early days. In what seemed a very short time, Port Stanley took on the appearance almost of a ghost town. Those who were able to do so arranged for their children to stay out of town—it was still possible to get out of Stanley over land. With almost all the children now on the farms, the town seemed that much greyer. Our Sunday School ceased functioning immediately the invasion happened; some of our regular attenders were moved out of Stanley, and others – the children of expatriates – left the Islands with their families within a few days. There wasn't a chance to have a last Sunday School meeting to say goodbye; by the first Sunday, almost all the children were gone, and those who remained were not allowed out by their parents. The uncertainty about what was going to happen in Stanley and also about how long it would be possible to move about freely gave the whole situation a great urgency. Whole families, as well as children on their own, went to the Camp. Sometimes I was approached by people about to leave and asked whether I would keep an eye on their home, or their freezer, or whatever. At that time nobody knew how prolonged their absence might be.

Although our Sunday School was closed, we were still able to hold our Sunday services in the Cathedral, and these were attended by large numbers of residents. The invasion had taken place just before Palm Sunday, as the church year moved towards its climax of Easter; a poignant contrast between the joy and exultation and hope of the Resurrection, and the bitter blow that had befallen our Islands. On Good Friday I was able to broadcast an Easter message to the Islands. (Though I did not know it at the time, it was my last broadcast message. Our radio facilities were withdrawn a few days later.) I was glad to be able to quote several examples of good humour and resilience, and to report that many local people had been quick to help in providing community services which had been disrupted by the arrival of the Argentines. It was a very personal message, because I was talking primarily to all those people scattered around the Islands with whom Iris and I had had wonderful times of fellowship.

My prayer for you all is that you will be strengthened for any test you may face, and that you will know the joy of sharing with others in difficult times; that you will be free from anxiety and put your trust in the Lord Jesus, whose victory we celebrate this weekend, who rose from the dead.

It was a prayer for myself and Iris too.

Many of those to whom I was broadcasting saw almost nothing of the fighting or even of the Argentines. The theatre of war was confined to several small and restricted locations, and in large areas of the Islands the residents never saw anybody in combat uniform. But they suffered in a different way. Many were sharing their homes with people who had left Stanley, and for the period of the invasion their lives were turned upside down as they stretched their resources to accommodate the influx of evacuees. More than that, they shared in the fears and uncertainties of those who had homes and families in the capital. They did not know, either, what the future held for them; whether the bombing would be extended to their farms, whether the area in which they lived would be the site of a major land battle, whether the Argentines would commandeer precious supplies of food and fuel. Communications between Port Stanley and Camp were minimal in the early days of the invasion and deteriorated as the weeks passed. It was a different war in much of the Camp, but also a terrible one.

I tried to encourage my listeners by reminding them, 'In Camp you have less to fear than in Stanley, and even here, there is nothing to be afraid of.' For myself I was able to say honestly that I felt little fear, apart from butterflies in the stomach. It was no less than the truth. From the morning of the invasion on, I was sustained by a conviction that whatever happened, I was going to come through this alive; that God was going to protect my life against anything that might come along. I believe that this was God speaking to me very specifically. I recalled the time that I had spent in hospital years before, when my life was despaired of. I was so seriously ill that my father, having visited me in hospital once, never came back; he could not bear to see me like that, and he was convinced I was going to die. God saved my life then; everything since had been a bonus. I had faced the possibility of death at that time and had experienced the power of God's strengthening and uplifting. I have not feared death since.

On Easter Sunday we had a service of hymns and readings in place of evensong. Once again the Cathedral was packed, but there was a note of sadness. Eleven people in the congregation had been ordered to leave the Islands within two days. We did not know when they would return, if ever. As the congregation left, I embraced each of them.

Hospital visiting continued to be a regular part of my work. On one occasion I visited an elderly lady, who had come to Port Stanley from Camp for treatment. Her husband was prevented from visiting her because of the invasion, and she was missing him badly.

'And how are you today, my dear?' I asked.

'Oh, I'm fine,' she said. Her voice was flat and

lifeless. She picked nervously at her blanket and tried to smile.

I looked hard at her. 'You're not really, though, are you. There's something up. Do you want to talk about it?'

She shrugged. 'Oh, it's all right. I'm just a bit tired.' As she spoke, a tear was welling up in her eye.

I held her hand. 'Please tell me.'

She choked back a sob. 'Padre, I don't mind what happens to me, I really don't. But I know it could get very bad here in Stanley.'

I was about to try to reassure her, but she continued: 'All I want is that whatever happens to me, I'm with my husband when it happens. Mr Bagnall, I want to go home. I want to be with him.' And she broke down.

It took only minutes to locate the doctor and tell him that his patient had expressed a desire to go home. He was willing to discharge her – she was being treated for a leg infection – and we worked out a plan. I made several telephone calls to people living outside Port Stanley, and we set up a chain of people, each of whom would pick the lady up at the appointed place and take her to the next pickup point for the next driver. The device worked wonderfully. She got home without any problems, and was with her husband a few hours after leaving hospital.

Daily life in Port Stanley took on the atmosphere of a military camp, which indeed it had become. The constant coming and going at the Airport soon became part of our lives, and we no longer stopped what we were doing to watch the latest Argentine Hercules C130 begin its long descent on to the runway. Helicopters were suddenly numerous; the football ground next to Government House was a landing site for them, and the constant ferrying in of fuel and weapons, which were then taken overland to scattered units around the town, was a noisy cause of distress to the elderly residents living nearby. Close to the football ground a rocket launcher had been installed, ominously pointing at the skies. All over Port Stanley, machine gun emplacements were being prepared, and on the hills behind the town, more powerful gun positions were being built.

We also became quickly used to the sight of soldiers in the streets. There were usually a few leaning against the Cathedral walls. I had not abandoned my usual practice of going into the vestry before church services and ringing the bell as loudly as I could. Quite frequently I emerged from the church to find several soldiers staring accusingly at me in a state of shock; the bell had taken them by surprise and their first thought had been that it was signalling a military retaliation against them.

The soldiers were disciplined in their attitude towards us. Initially, they were under orders not to carry guns into the shops; then they were banned from going into the shops at all. It was quite common to find soldiers hovering near the stores, asking local residents to buy cigarettes for them, rather like children on the look out for sympathetic adults to help them contravene the age limit on tobacco purchases. They also asked for help in buying chocolate, biscuits and other foodstuffs. Many of the soldiers seemed to be badly equipped and underfed.

The shopkeepers hid their supplies of cigarettes from the Argentines. One never knew how difficult it might be to replace stock when it was exhausted. Better to keep luxuries for the Islanders. So the soldiers were sometimes disappointed.

But in those early days, food was generally plentiful. Whether it would remain so was one of our worries. We grow our own food, not simply because we are enthusiastic gardeners (some of us are not!), but because it is vital to do so if we are to have enough to eat. With another 10,000 men arriving or due to arrive on the Islands, how would they be fed?

At the Deanery we saw quite a lot of the Argentine soldiers, because they took over my garage and installed two oil-fired ovens in it. It became one of their kitchens. Although many of the troops appeared to be underfed, the group in charge of the kitchen was responsible for the organisation and distribution of food, so they did not go short themselves. We became used to the sight of young soldiers preparing quantities of steaks. The aroma of these succulent dishes was hidden from us by the stench of oil fumes issuing from the garage. I went into the garage one day to look for something, and found that a number of things I had been storing there were missing — including my fishing rod. I protested to one of the non-commissioned officers, and eventually I got my fishing rod and some of my other possessions back.

Near the garage there was an armed guard post. There were soldiers permanently watching, weapons at the ready, and we became used to their gaze following us as we left the house. They were stationed there because one of the buildings behind the Deanery had been taken over as a supply centre and army premises. Not long after the guard post had been set up I walked over to it one day with my camera, and took a photograph of the soldier on duty. He became quite agitated about this, and began to protest; but by then I had my picture. I smiled, waved at him, and moved away.

Relations with the troops were always awkward. They had been told to be civil to us, but they were mistrustful of us and obviously scared. Even very early in the occupation, before the steadily approaching Task Force had made the Argentines very nervous indeed, it was usual to find even small courtesies misinterpreted. We felt very sorry for the Argentine youngsters, and on Good Friday, as Iris was taking a tray of Hot Cross Buns from the oven, we saw through the window a guard at his post looking particularly depressed. On the spur of the moment I buttered one of the hot buns and put it into a paper bag. Then I went off to where the soldier was standing.

He looked at me doubtfully as I approached, and as I offered him the bun he tensed and clutched his rifle.

'Sweet bread!' I said encouragingly, in my best Spanish. The soldier grimaced and waved me away with his rifle. I tried again: 'Sweet bread!' The response was the same. In the end I shrugged my shoulders and walked away, munching the bun myself. When I looked back from the house he was still standing on guard, his rifle held defensively in front of him, angry and mistrustful.

Life under enemy occupation had its humorous aspects, but it also had its sad ones. In particular, the plight of the elderly and the sick was very distressing. Visiting and comforting them was high on my list of priorities; often housebound and out of touch with the latest developments, they needed to be told what was going on and reassured. Also, as the occupation wore on, people continued to leave. The population of Stanley shrank to about half the size as residents found ways to get out to the outlying farms, or took the plane out from the Islands altogether. One of the saddest of my new duties since the invasion was saying goodbye to people.

It was while I was saying goodbye to a group flying out that I was invited to meet General Mario Benjamin Menendez.

7: General Menendez

> British sovereignty over the Islands rests
> on a secure historical and legal foundation.
>
> *Paper No. 170/82, 'Falkland Islands:*
> *Britain's search for a negotiated settlement'.*
> *Central Office of Information, London.*

> There were deep roots to Argentina's
> attitude to the 'Malvinas'.
>
> *'Report' of Lord Franks's Committee of*
> *Inquiry.*

The Argentine officer on the other side of the street
glanced incuriously at our little group. Then he took a
longer look. He was staring at me.

It was Tuesday 13 April. Tuesday was departure
day for Buenos Aires; if you had the money and
wanted to leave the Islands you turned up at the
LADE offices in Stanley and were taken out in convoy
to the Airport. I had come with this group, who were
leaving, to say goodbye. Some were going because
they had only been staying temporarily anyway;

others were residents over a longer period, leaving not because they wanted to but because they had to do so for various reasons. There were a good many who had already left against their will; all the senior Government officers had gone, and others who had been refused permission to stay by the Argentines. This group was the latest to go.

The Argentine crossed over and came up to where I was standing. He indicated my clerical collar and smiled.

'Mr Bagnall?' His English was very good. He sounded a brisk, efficient sort of man.

'I'm Harry Bagnall,' I replied.

He smiled pleasantly. 'I am Comodoro Blumer-Reve.'

He was a slim, tall man, in his forties, with a fair complexion and receding hair. His manner was slightly reticent, almost deferential, though he had the assured authority and bearing of a senior military officer.

'General Menendez wishes to see you.' The announcement was made calmly. It was not a threat. Nevertheless, I was momentarily disorientated. The bright day seemed suddenly chill.

'Very well; I would be willing to meet him.'

'Good,' smiled Blumer-Reve.

'When?'

'What would be a suitable time?' he asked. His manner was courteous, as if inviting a new acquaintance in for a drink.

'Tomorrow morning would be convenient.'

'Well then, I suggest that you make your way to Government House tomorrow, and I will inform General Menendez that you will be coming.'

'No,' I said sharply.

The Argentine looked surprised. 'I beg your pardon?'

'I will not walk past your guards,' I said. 'I do not speak their language, and I do not wish to push through their lines without being able to explain where I am going. I am willing to meet General Menendez, but I will not go alone.'

'Very well. Tomorrow I will escort you to Government House.' After fixing a time and a rendezvous, the Comodoro nodded amiably to the others in the group and went on his way.

By the time we reached the airport, I had almost forgotten the incident. The place was a frenzy of activity. Shouted Spanish commands rose above the noise of the idling aeroplane engines as a squad of young Argentines marched by. Behind us, a group of soldiers were manhandling large steel containers into a waiting van. The airport was full of people and noise as ground vehicles arrived and left, and large military aircraft taxied to unloading points. People were running to and fro. The sheer size of the operation was staggering. Our small airport had never witnessed anything like it.

Our little group stood by the LADE Airline departure point. We didn't say much to each other. Everybody was busy with his or her own thoughts.

We had to step back suddenly as another squad marched past, close to where we were standing. They were young, like most of the soldiers in Port Stanley; eyes fixed rigidly ahead, marching determinedly, not quite in step. The Argentines were obviously using large numbers of raw recruits. The officer with them barked orders, and they headed off towards a pile of cartons which were waiting to be loaded on to a truck. I watched them go.

'Well,' I remarked to the others, 'with all these uniforms about the place – at least there are enough porters to go round now!'

It wasn't a very funny joke; the others grinned politely. It was at that precise moment, however, that several Argentine soldiers appeared, crisp and genial, and with beaming smiles insisted on carrying the luggage to the plane. We trooped off, the soldiers making conversation and generally trying to be friendly, the rest of us at least enjoying a leisurely, unencumbered stroll. The policy of befriending us and presenting themselves in the most favourable light possible had certain practical benefits so far as we were concerned.

The next day, Government House was guarded by Argentine soldiers as Blumer-Reve and I got out of his Landrover at the front door. I could see clearly the damage that the house had suffered in the battle a few days earlier – bullet-holes in the walls and smashed windows were visible. We entered unchallenged. I was glad I had an official escort. As we entered the building, several officers standing near the door greeted us. Blumer-Reve introduced me to them. Names were repeated to me which I only half heard and did not recognise. We exchanged a few awkward, formal handshakes. After some minutes Blumer-Reve excused himself and another officer I did not know took me to the office of General Menendez.

It was a room I recognised. So far as I remembered, it had hardly been altered by its new occupant. Visiting Rex Hunt, I had been in it once or twice; I had once been received there by his predecessor, Governor Parker; but I didn't know the room well. It was the Governor's working office. Some of the old pictures still hung on the walls, and the furniture was as I remembered it. There was one new object; a very special hat, rather like a large opera hat, made out of a furry fabric with a rosette and feather attached to one side. I recognised it as part of an antique Argentine dress uniform. It occupied a special place, like a sporting trophy, presumably an emblem of Menendez' new office as Governor of the Islands, a faintly ridiculous badge of authority. The owner of the hat greeted me at the door. General Menendez was not a tall man; he was slim, and his dark hair was severely brushed back from his face and neatly parted in the centre. He acknowledged me courteously and gestured me to a chair. We sat facing each other, a table between us.

'May I offer you tea or coffee?'

I asked for tea, and the General gave an order in Spanish. A few minutes later a tea-tray was brought in by a soldier and placed on the table between us. I recognised the servant. It was the young Argentine who had been at the back of the Cathedral at Evensong on Palm Sunday. I smiled discreetly at him and he flickered a response. It was not a good time to greet each other further.

I stared at the well-cared for, authoritative invader. His face was lined like many South Americans' faces; his army career had obviously not been spent wholly behind an office desk. *What am I to say to this man?* I asked myself. *What is his attitude to me?* I found myself noticing that his feet were small.

Menendez began to speak, in careful, precise English, clasping his hands in front of him. As he spoke, he rocked slightly backwards and forwards from the hips, emphasising the points he was making. He had the assured manner of somebody who knows that because he is in charge, he can afford to give respect and courtesy.

He was polite but unsmiling, and spent no time asking how we were managing in the new situation or about the community in general, but launched into what had every appearance of being a prepared speech.

'The Argentine people have repossessed the Malvinas Islands,' he stated. I permitted myself a secret smile at the word 'repossessed' – I preferred the word 'invaded'. Menendez' rhetoric carried on in full flight. 'The Islands are ours; we have reoccupied them. It is not certain exactly what will happen in the future; but there will be gradual change. The education system will continue for a time. There will be two languages in use at the present time; eventually there will be only one.'

He continued in this vein for several minutes. He was explaining – expounding – the Argentine position, like a preacher delivering a sermon. There was little I could say in response and no opportunity to interrupt his flow. The speech contained very little actual information, but a considerable amount of exhortation.

He appeared to come to the end of his prepared statement and moved on to a topic which directly concerned me. 'There is to be an important visitor,' he announced. 'Bishop Cutts. He will be visiting the Islands.'

I looked at him in dismay. The proposed visit, of which I had heard rumours, was – if those rumours were true – potentially a highly delicate problem. Bishop Cutts was the Bishop of Argentina and Eastern South America. When in 77/78 he was appointed Archbishop's Episcopal Commissary in the Falkland Islands there had been considerable resentment in Port Stanley because it looked as though his appointment represented an extension of Argentine influence over the Falklands. But by the warmth of his personality and the evidence of his work, he had made great headway in overcoming much of the prejudice of the congregation and being accepted. The invasion had brought all this to an end. It was widely reported in the Press that he intended to lead a deputation to the Islands, made up of Argentines who would convince us that it was good to be Argentine, and apply pressure on the Island's churchgoers to consider the merits of life under Argentine rule.

I had no way of knowing whether or not the rumours were true. But in any case they had already been a source of considerable embarrassment to me. The Islanders were in no mood to listen to the Bishop, and had spoken to me and telephoned me to assure me that they wanted nothing to do with his deputation, or the Church itself for that matter if the visit was allowed to go ahead. I had already cabled the Bishop and asked him not to come. We were bitterly opposed to such a visit, it was completely inappropriate to the mood of the population, and the visit would be unwelcome. I had also cabled the Archbishop of Canterbury and requested him to make the situation quite clear, and Dr Runcie had responded immediately by broadcasting a statement asserting his own authority over the Church in the Falkland Islands, and also stating that I was his chaplain.

I tried to express this as clearly as I could to Menendez.

'I have heard rumours of this visit,' I answered. 'He is not welcome. The visit of the Bishop at this time would be of no value to you and would do untold damage to my work. While I might welcome him into my home as a friend from former years I will not offer him a platform for his views. It would put me beyond the trust of the people.'

Menendez shrugged. I suspected that he knew nothing about the work of the Anglican Church in South America, and he gave no impression that he found the subject anything other than boring. 'The arrangements are not mine. I have merely been informed of them. You must make preparations for this visit.' He rocked forward as he enunciated each word. His manner was not aggressive; it was as if the whole discussion bored him. There was no point in pressing the point further.

I sipped my tea. Menendez was not drinking. The cups were the old Government House ones, with the British royal crest on the side and the saucers. It was strange. I was sitting with the General who commanded the forces which had invaded my country, and he was giving me tea out of crockery that carried the Queen's crest. For a brief moment it almost recalled other conversations and other meetings over that same crockery. But that was before April 1st 1982. A long time ago, it seemed.

Menendez sat back in his chair. 'Do you want to ask me any questions?'

There didn't seem a great deal to say. The initial edicts had assured us of freedom of worship, and there were no indications that there would be any long-term interference with the work of the Cathedral or that my pastoral work would be subject to official scrutiny. Then I thought of the ensigns which hung in the Cathedral; a Union Jack belonging to the earliest Falklands Defence Force, the ensign of the *Achilles* which had fought in the Battle of the River Plate, and an ensign presented by Christchurch, Port Stanley, Ontario. It seemed suddenly extremely important that these flags should be left undisturbed.

'In the Cathedral,' I said, 'there are some British flags. Will those be removed?'

Menendez looked at me levelly. 'Do you want them removed?'

'No,' I answered swiftly. 'They are battle honours.'

Menendez raised his eyebrows. I continued, 'They are from previous events.'

'You wish for them to stay,' repeated the General.

I nodded.

'Very well,' Menendez stated flatly. 'They will stay.'

I nodded my thanks. The subject was at an end, and so, apparently was the meeting. The General stood up; I stood up; I left and made my way out.

8: Taking stock

All the Argentines have to do is honour
UN Security Council Resolution 502.

Prime Minister Margaret Thatcher.

I was walking along Ross Road when I became aware
of somebody waving a greeting from a car. It was a
military Mercedes in khaki camouflage paint, with
two men sitting in the front. As the car passed I
looked again at the man who had waved, and recognised the sleek figure of General Menendez.

I did not wave back. In the Falklands, waving is a
pleasant greeting much used by us. In the course of a
five-minute walk along the street one waves several
times as various friends and acquaintances go by, and
they wave back. In common with most of the Islanders
I knew, I limited this greeting to our own people
during the occupation. I was quite prepared to be civil
to the Argentines; I even had the occasional joke with
those I knew reasonably well. But a wave of the hand
was a special greeting in Port Stanley, and one which
we wanted to keep for ouselves at a time when we
needed all the morale-boosting we could find.

I nodded a greeting, but Menendez' car was already

some distance past. He often waved to me during the occupation, and the most enthusiastic response he ever got from me was a brief nod and sometimes a polite smile. I doubt whether he even noticed. It was part of his policy to be friendly with as many Islanders as he could, itself a part of his wider strategy of removing unnecessary barriers between himself and the Islands he had been sent to govern; he selected his personal staff, for example, only from the English-speaking soldiers. His commitment to this conciliatory approach diminished markedly as events continued.

The day of my interview with him had marked the end of the first fortnight of Argentine occupation. It had been the strangest two weeks of my life. I had discovered in the middle of it that God is the same in the middle of war as he is in peacetime; that he calls his people to be faithful wherever they are and whatever circumstances they are in. We had seen his unchanging care in our own lives and in the lives of other people. We had proved him to be what he claimed to be.

One frail lady, a little over five feet in height and now very elderly, is one of our most faithful church attenders, despite the fact that she finds it difficult to get around easily now she is older. She is a lovely lady, born in the Islands, and now lives near the Cathedral –she is also the sister of our organist. She is one person who checks the time regularly by looking at the Cathedral clock through her window, so I always try to remember to keep the clock wound properly. I would hate to let Mrs Stacey down. I always enjoy spending time with her. She is rather formal with me, and I think she has high expectations of how clergymen should behave – she looks faintly shocked if I make her laugh or tease her. 'Oh! I'm surprised at *you*, Padre!' is her standard reproachful response.

She was one of the first people I visited after the invasion, and I was struck then by her resilience – she simply shrugged her shoulders as if to say, well, let's get on and see what this situation has to teach us. I made a point of visiting her at least twice a week after that. As the situation deteriorated and later there were planes overhead, Mrs Stacey took a lively interest in what was happening, and even though she was not very mobile, she always made the effort to get to the window to see the action. During the nightly curfew it was thought necessary to move her into a more substantial house – her own was in an exposed position and wasn't very bullet-proof – she spent the nights in her nephew's house where one or two other neighbours were also sheltering. It was quite remarkable to see how, when things got noisy outside, Mrs Stacey remained the coolest of them all. She is a delightful, indomitable lady, and a wonderful testimony to God's comfort and strengthening in difficult circumstances. In hospital at present with a painful disability, she is still tranquil and composed whenever I visit her.

In my visiting during those early days I saw many similar examples of courage and bravery. Although the official line being taken by the Argentines was that the Islands were about to enter a period of unparalleled peace and prosperity under their benevolence, the soldiers parading on the streets and the increasing evidence of military build-up told a different story. The Argentines were clearly resigned to the fact that sooner or later there was going to be a military confrontation. The spectacle of many of the gun positions and heavy artillery being located on the perimeter of Stanley itself was far from encouraging.

When the action happened, it was going to be happening very near to home. As time passed, there was a good deal of indiscipline on the part of the troops which the officers could not always control. There were thefts from houses, random interference with the peaceful activities of the residents, and occasional sporadic firing of guns in anger, frustration or boredom. It made life very tense: like living in a powder-keg near a spluttering flame.

The life of the Cathedral had changed dramatically when the invasion took place, but we were able to carry on the usual chores. The Church was kept clean by volunteers. As the cooler weather was approaching in April, there was not much that needed to be done in the grounds – we normally cut the grass in the Cathedral grounds only in the summer months. So we managed to keep the Cathedral 'housekeeping' under control.

As the situation changed, so did my job. For a start, it was immediately reduced. Before the invasion, I was responsible for the whole of the Islands. During the occupation I was restricted to Port Stanley. Even when a death occurred in a farm sixteen miles away, I was not allowed to go there to conduct the funeral, neither would the Argentines allow the body to be brought into Stanley for burial. In the event, I had to tell the farm manager by telephone what to do. The deceased was an elderly man, a resident of Stanley, who had left after the invasion to live with relatives at Fitzroy and had died there. The manager brought a copy of the Book of Common Prayer to the telephone and I went through the service with him, explaining what had to be done. Fortunately I had every confidence in him – he was a member of my congregation, from one of our most faithful families. But the incident highlighted for me the limitations I now had to work with.

Also the quantity of administration, which takes a large amount of any clergyman's time, was dramatically reduced. It dwindled to practically nothing in the new situation in Port Stanley, and in its place was simply the bare bones of ministry. Worship in the Cathedral had been reduced; consequently the amount of preparation dropped. The cycle of business and administrative meetings, church councils and so on, abruptly stopped; a further freeing of my time. I was left simply with the task of caring for people and exercising my pastoral ministry, and on this I concentrated. Those unique weeks were a high spot in my ministry. Visiting people in their homes, sharing and counselling with them, now took all my time. We are so burdened with the trappings of ministry in the usual way of things that we can lose sight of our priorities, and I am grateful to the Lord for taking the trappings away and directing me to what I should be doing for him during that time.

The conversations I had each day while out visiting were mainly practical and morale-boosting – there was a great deal to be done advising people, and as a minister I had some opportunities to make representations to the authorities. The Monsignor was also in that position, and between us we were able to help with a number of practical problems people were facing. One thing we were able to help particularly with was the squashing of rumours, because as clergymen we had some access to official channels. Rumours grew and spread very rapidly. It was said that a heavily-guarded vessel moored in the harbour was holding prisoners of war from South Georgia. Investigation proved the rumour false. Later, it was said that a captured British pilot was being ill-treated; I was able to ascertain that the story was almost certainly false. It was easy to allow incidents to become distorted. One or two people gave way to panic, and for their peace of mind and that of the community, their fears had to be laid to rest. We had enough to worry about with real danger on our doorsteps, without wasting time on imagined perils.

Many simply wanted to talk, to share their fears and their worries. And every now and then I would find myself talking to someone who wanted to ask deeper questions – 'Where is God in all this? What does it mean, why has he allowed it to happen?'

If my job had changed, so had the role of the Cathedral in the life of the town. At the beginning of the occupation, the attendances increased dramatically. I found that people wanted to talk to me in the street, that there was a desire to identify with the Cathedral. I was very glad of this, because it gave me opportunities to make contact with many people who might have previously avoided me, and also to get into conversation. It broke the ice, and it broke down barriers which, in many cases, remain broken to this day. In addition, sharing the experience of the occupation with the Kelpers did I think earn forgiveness for the fact that I was an expatriate, there merely to do a job and in due course leave. Nowadays the question asked in Port Stanley is often not 'Were you born here? Are you a Kelper?', but 'Were you here during the occupation?' As a Yorkshireman – and consequently heir to a great heritage! – I can sympathise with the strong bond that joins the Kelper community together, but I am glad that one by-product of the tragedy of the invasion has been an increased measure of acceptance in Port Stanley. I hope that my ministry will benefit from it.

We also began to develop a new community spirit concerning the future. During that first fortnight, I had a conversation with somebody about the advisability of planning for the time when the British arrived, so that we could ask that certain matters be negotiated with the Argentines as part of their surrender – undertakings to remove their Alsatian dogs, for example, which they had brought into the Islands (they were savage-looking brutes, and more than a dozen of them patrolled Argentine posts near the Deanery), and to provide maps of the minefields. The idea of a committee to plan for such things did not work out, and in any case all our problems were dealt with by the British forces who demanded, for example, minefield maps from the defeated Argentines. But the fact that the conversation took place at all indicated that there was a resolve, even in the early days, to actively plan for the future.

I was curious to know what Padres the Argentines had brought with them. There were about seven, and I met most of them as time went by. One, a young man probably just out of seminary, was a typical Argentine nationalist, aloof and remote. He ignored me until he discovered that I was in charge of the Cathedral, and for one morning he was quite civil to me as I showed him round the building.

Quite the opposite was a very elderly priest who must have been in retirement. He had presumably come as a volunteer out of concern for the troops. He was often to be seen handing rosaries to the soldiers; he had a large quantity of them, which he produced at every opportunity. Another priest was quite different again; looking more like a soldier than a padre, he sported a Castro beard and lived in the Upland Goose, where his overbearing attitude to his fellow-residents lost him any popularity he started with.

The clergyman I had seen on the day of the invasion, who wore an eye-patch, seemed to be a very genuine man. I know that he was doing a good deal of counselling among the soldiers, and was holding catechism classes. He approached me several times enquiring whether I had any Spanish Scriptures, and I was able to supply him with one or two Bibles and New Testaments.

It was exciting, and an answer to our prayers, to know that the Word of God was being preached among the young Argentines, who, apart from those who found their way into our services and those of the Monsignor, were out of reach of our ministry.

We entered the third week of April, our third of occupation, having come to terms to some extent with what had befallen us. The soldiers were at least attempting to be considerate, their officers were openly conciliatory, and nobody had been killed. The Task Force was steaming towards us, the British were on their way. The weather was still beautiful, an extension of summer providentially continuing and delaying the onset of the bitter winter seas which were the factor that would eventually determine the strategy adopted by the Task Force. We began to feel some stability in the situation. I took stock and looked forward.

But nobody could predict how things would turn out even from one week to the next. Events were moving too fast. The situation, far from stabilising, was in reality sliding into the next phase.

Interlude

By the end of April, international opinion had turned against Argentina. The European Economic Community imposed trade sanctions. The United States risked its relationship with South America and backed Britain. General Haig's efforts at mediation appeared to be stalemated. On 23 April, the government in London advised British nationals living in Argentina to leave the country.

On 25 April, a British landing party which had detached from the main Task Force retook the Falkland Island dependency of South Georgia. It was a famous victory. The British commander invited the Argentine commander to dinner after the battle, and the next day in the House of Commons Margaret Thatcher described the operation to Members of Parliament as a skilled and professional piece of work.

The Task Force had set sail ('Impossible!' an Argentine officer had said to me laughingly, earlier in the month. 'That would be a ridiculous escalation of the conflict. A Task Force?'). Now it had arrived. In the waters around the Islands, they were moving into position, ships loaded with men, arms and fighter planes.

And still the incredible weather continued. 'The only good thing the Argies brought with them,' it was said, as the onset of winter was delayed by day after day of sunshine and winds that were tolerable. I harvested my potatoes and looked for somewhere to hide them. Food was likely to become scarcer.

The Argentines painted the Post Office in their national colours of blue and white. They also added two enormous rosettes, which they erected on either side of the main door about ten feet from the ground. The job took them several hours, and when it was finished the Post Office was a splendid monument to Argentina. The effort was wasted. Within hours, a strong Falkland wind had begun, and the rosettes were blown off the walls and disappeared.

We continued our work in the parish, visiting, helping where we could.

I had been at the Upland Goose Hotel, talking with others about the situation in Stanley, the South Georgia victory, the prospects for the next few days, and the arrival of the Task Force. It was evening. My day's work was finished. No more could be done that night anyway: residents were ordered to keep to their houses after dark.

Before going in, I paused at the Deanery door, looking out across the dark water of the harbour and beyond, over the blackening ocean. I could hear Spanish voices laughing a few yards down Ross Road, and the scrape of army boots on the pavement. The familiar smell of peat smoke curled from my chimney; inside, Iris would be cooking our supper. I stood a while longer, staring at the sea. Somewhere, out there in two hundred miles of water, the ships were waiting: the *Hermes*, the *Invincible*, the frigates, the destroyers, the small ships, the big ships; old grey battle-vessels already under notice for the scrapyard, and luxury liners and merchant cargo ships pressed into duty and hurriedly fitted out with the trappings of war. They lay somewhere, in formation, with helicopters buzzing round them like flies. Aboard them were thousands of men: men who were waiting, too. Sleek jets strapped to the carrier decks groaning in the swaying of the slapping sea. Sergeants below decks roaring commands to ranks of men trying to shave seconds off their reload time. Paras hard as nails, crisply-turned-out Gurkhas, the Welshmen, the Irishmen, the Scotsmen, the Northerners and the Southerners. Waiting and watching, patrolling the Total Exclusion Zone; in my imagination, a pattern of shadows on the wild and restless sea.

9: The end of the honeymoon

Wild shooting was heard at night when guards shot at every cat, shadow, and even each other. Houses were riddled with bullets without warning. Suddenly no one was safe; yet, miraculously, no one was injured.

Harry Bagnall writing in 'Intercon', the magazine of the Intercontinental Church Society, Winter 1982.

If anybody living in Port Stanley had been lulled into a sense of complacency by the attitude of the Argentines in the first month of occupation, that illusion was shattered by the events of May.

By this time Monsignor Spraggon and I had acquired a role as tacitly acknowledged leaders in the eyes of a large part of the community. The government officers had been expelled from the Islands, and there was nobody else left. Some government employees had been meeting together earlier in April, and had written to London to recommend that the civilian population should somehow be evacuated before the final onslaught. Rex

Hunt responded to the suggestion in a broadcast in which he said that he believed the people did not want this, and I think he had read the mood of Port Stanley quite accurately.

The Monsignor and I, partly because we were non-combatant and partly because of our position as ministers, were being called on increasingly when there were problems to be resolved or issues to be negotiated with the Argentines. This was rather different from the suggestion I received by telephone somewhat earlier in the occupation, when a voice known to me said, 'Well, it's up to you now, you have to be our leader; everbody's gone, you're the only person left to give a lead.' He then proceeded to tell me exactly what I had to do in my new role, and his suggestions were in the area of political campaigning, representations to London, and other areas which I felt were quite outside my responsibility. I declined the invitation . . .

Of course, many other people in the community came forward to contribute skills of leadership and special abilities. Mention should be made of the people who volunteered to help at the hospital as ambulance drivers and be stretcher bearers or firemen or help in other ways if needed.

Another source of leadership for the community came in the area of civil defence. Organisers emerged in each part of Stanley, who divided the area up into regions and selected brick or stone dwellings in each area as safe dwellings and shelters.

One of the ways in which I and Monsignor found ourselves in a new situation of leadership was the increasing need to make representations to the authorities on behalf of the community. There were complaints to be reported, grievances to be registered, questions that needed answers. There was increasing concern for the safety of the empty houses vacated by those who had left Stanley. In the early days of the occupation the soldiers had been given strict instructions to protect property, but when the Total Exclusion Zone came into force at the end of April and the ships of the Task Force arrived in its waters, there was a change in the attitude and behaviour of the troops. Whereas previously the civil administration of Menendez and his staff had secured their good behaviour, now in this increasingly military situation the officers in the field were the chief authority. We began to look at the soldiers in a new light, and when I left the house, I sometimes glanced nervously at the guards lying flat on their stomachs behind their guns on the school roof, watching all that went on in our vicinity.

I had previously made arrangements with the Argentines for soldiers to be billeted in the Church Hall. The high rent I extracted made a virtue out of necessity, but I had been adamant that the Cathedral was not to be used for defensive purposes. Nevertheless, as the occupation wore on, defensive positions were erected in front of the Cathedral, or at its corner, and men were postioned behind them. Sometimes armed guards could be seen there at night. Whatever was going on, the strategic importance of the Cathedral was being checked out by the soldiers, which was the very thing I least wanted.

I made protests to Blumer-Reve, and the defences were dismantled and the armed guards removed. But in the next few weeks they reappeared, and my protests were less effective. Promises of action were followed up after long delays. There was no total withdrawal from the Cathedral vicinity. It acquired the feel of a place earmarked for military purposes; the soldiers walking round had a proprietary air, as if sizing up exactly where the various guns and sandbags would be best placed when the time came. Token apologies and temporary removal of defences made little difference. It was obvious that the civil authorities, who were the ones I had access to, were no longer running things. We were not merely an occupied territory under new management. We were an occupied territory awaiting the first moves of a liberating military force which was patrolling the seas around us.

Nevertheless I continued to make our views known to the authorities as energetically as I could.

On 29 April, the day when the Total Exclusion Zone came into force, I received a terse message from the hospital. The Haines family—the two doctors, Daniel and Hilary, and their three children—were being taken away. Dr Daniel Haines was the Senior Medical Officer at the Hospital, an ordained man as well who had assisted me as Curate when he arrived in Port Stanley. I leapt into my Landrover and raced to the Hospital, only to see the Haines's vehicle leaving the premises with the family and an Argentine police officer. I could not make the vehicle stop, so I followed it to the Police Station.

As the two vehicles pulled up, I switched off my engine, jumped to the ground and went over to the Haines's to find out what was going on. Before I could speak to them, a senior army officer stepped between us. My protests were unheeded, I could not persuade him to let me speak to them.

A few yards away the Monsignor was standing. Together we demanded information from officials. All we could find out was that they were taking the

Haines's to an unspecified destination. We discovered that there had been hardly any notice given.

There was obviously not very much to be done there. We left the Police Station. The Haines family were still standing in a group when when we left, waiting to find out what was going to happen. We went straight to Blumer-Reve's office at the Secretariat Building. Captain Hussey, the Argentine naval officer, was with him. By this time I had established a reasonable relationship with Blumer-Reve, who was the person I most often found myself being referred to when I made representations to the military authorities on behalf of my parishioners.

'What is going on?' we demanded. 'Why are the Haines family being taken from the Hospital? Have they broken the law?'

Blumer-Reve looked embarrassed as he and Captain Hussey greeted us formally. He answered our questions quietly, his characteristically deliberate enunciation emphasising each point.

'No, it is an order which has been issued. Be assured, they will not be harmed.'

'Why was it necessary to take them away at such short notice? Their children are frightened.'

Both men seemed agitated. I had the impression that they were not happy to be involved in the arrest of the Haines's, and as we continued to demand explanations Blumer-Reve's manner edged towards anger. He kept himself in control, however, and seemed genuinely anxious to be as informative as he could be in the circumstances.

'The children will be safer where they are going. The family is being taken to a farm on West Falkland.'

This at least was a relief. Much of the horror of the

situation lay in the fact that the Haines family, the hospital staff and ourselves did not know what purpose lay behind their arrest.

'Why was it necessary to do this? They have done nothing wrong. They are doctors.'

Captain Hussey explained. 'There is a list. There are those in the town who must be taken away for their safety. They will not be harmed.'

I looked at Blumer-Reve, then at the Captain. Neither of them seemed particularly happy about the situation.

'I want to see the list.'

'That is not possible,' said Hussey smoothly. 'We do not have a copy.'

'At least the names,' I insisted. 'Who are these people who must be moved?'

Blumer-Reve smiled ruefully. 'I cannot tell you all the names. I do not have the list.'

'Is my name on that list?' I asked abruptly.

Blumer-Reve frowned. 'I don't know, Mr Bagnall. All I can say to you is, do not go far away from home. You understand?'

'Are we to be under house arrest?' I demanded. 'We are already forbidden to move more than 200 metres in any direction.'

Blumer-Reve shook his head with an exaggerated air of patience. 'Do not go far from home,' he repeated.

The telephone rang, and Hussey picked up the receiver and spoke in a low voice, frowning as he listened to the person at the other end. Our conversation was punctuated by several more calls, which seemed to be in some way related to what had happened to the Haines family. Each brief telephone call seemed to add to the irritation of the two men.

We tried to persuade them to rescind the detention order. We pointed out that the action they had taken in removing the Haines family – who were not only well-liked and respected in the community, but also represented a continuation of the patterns of life that had existed before the invasion – was unnecessarily harsh, calculated either deliberately or by lack of foresight to terrify the people arrested and to spread panic among the population. We said to them that so far, there had been no violence from the community, the residents of the Islands had by and large been purely passive in opposition. All that might change if they persisted in sudden arrests. If it were absolutely necessary to make arrests, was there no other way it might be done, to prevent distress and anger in the community?

Blumer-Reve suddenly looked sharply at the Monsignor. 'Yes, that is true. And you yourselves have things to answer for.'

We looked at him perplexedly. 'What do you mean?'

He stared at us. 'It is true, is it not, that you have secret meetings?'

There was a pause. Captain Hussey, who had been a bystander in the conversation, was now watching us intently.

'That is not true,' said the Monsignor.

'We have heard otherwise,' Blumer-Reve said softly. 'There have been meetings among the community. Secret meetings. It is known, Monsignor, that people have come to your home in secrecy.'

The Monsignor reacted explosively. He almost hit the roof. 'Are we now to be under suspicion?' he demanded. 'For what reason?'

The two officers were visibly taken aback by his

reaction, which was understandable. No edict had forbidden meeting together, and the Argentines knew perfectly well that people were meeting in different houses; but there was no attempt to conceal the fact. There was no underground movement so far as I knew. It was all in the open. Blumer-Reve and Hussey attempted to conciliate the Monsignor, and the atmosphere of the meeting returned to its previous strained politeness.

But we got no further in our demand for information about the Haines family or their destination. It was useless. They were quite inflexible. We left at four o'clock, frustrated and anxious. As I made my way home, I passed the Police Station. The Haines's and the police accompanying them were nowhere to be seen. Presumably they were on their way out to West Falkland to whatever farm had been chosen for their exile.

A pick-up truck squealed to a stop. I stepped back and watched. It was open at the back. I glanced in curiously, but from the shelter of my own vehicle. There was a rolled tarpaulin lying across the floor of the truck. Protruding from the tarpaulin were a pair of shoes. Then they moved, and I realised they were not just shoes but feet. There was somebody rolled up in the tarpaulin, and his or her legs were tied. The hands were also manacled to the rear of the cab.

Thoroughly concerned now, I hovered in the background and waited to see what was happening. The truck was quickly surrounded by armed guards. The driver jumped from the cab and came round the back. Having released the hands, he pulled the tarpaulin aside and roughly pulled a man in civilian clothes out. I watched in relief as the man clambered upright, wincing as he stretched his legs – for a moment I had thought it might be a corpse in the truck.

There was an exchange of Spanish. I breathed a little easier. It wasn't an English voice. Perhaps it was an Argentine soldier under arrest. But I wasn't sure. As the man was taken into the Police Station, the Argentines standing around him kept their guns levelled. Was this a British secret serviceman? There had been rumours that the SBS were already on East Falkland. And why would an Argentine soldier be wearing civilian dress?

The senior police officer grunted something in Spanish; the prisoner replied in the same language. They went inside. I was partly reassured. Perhaps I was over-reacting. I hoped so. I went home and told Iris what had happened.

That evening, a blackout and curfew were imposed on Port Stanley. The air traffic over the next few days became noticeably quieter. The helicopters were less active. It was obvious that the imposition of the Total Exclusion Zone at this date had an immediate effect.

We were very anxious about our safety in the event of air attacks, and an energetic civil defence programme was spontaneously organised by the residents, though it had the approval of the Argentines. When the blackout and curfew were imposed, it became a regular pattern of life for people living in timber houses to sleep in a designated safe house. (Our safe house for the last three weeks of the occupation was the Upland Goose Hotel. Iris and I began spending the hours of curfew there together with a number of others.) As the curfew was, by the end of the occupation, from 4 p.m. to 8.30 a.m., the experience was a new one for many of us, and the sharing of meals and other resources brought a new fellowship into our community life. One aspect of this which gave me tremendous pleasure was the experience of seeing members of my church who had never been particularly vocal about their faith, who were now speaking openly to others about the Lord; and there were other Christians known to me who were able to share their peace and assurance in the face of danger with others, and to explain how they came by it.

Two days after the arrest of the Haines family, we were woken up early by firing outside. We stood in the doorway and looked out across the harbour towards the Airport. Enormous explosions were shaking the ground, and thick columns of smoke were ascending into the moonless, overcast sky. The early morning darkness was split repeatedly by brilliant flashes. The faint drone of aircraft seemed impossibly high overhead; the Argentine gun positions were stuttering away on all sides. It was almost five o'clock on the morning of May 1st, and the British were bombing Port Stanley Airport.

It was so dark that we did not see much of the first action, but we saw a great deal of air combat later in the morning as the British came in with a Harrier attack to finish the job off. They flew in, wave after wave of them, each wave separated from the next only by seconds; they kept at a ceiling over the ground artillery, coming in so fast, with a white vapour trail streaming behind and a mighty roar of jets, that they were gone again almost before we realised they were there. The Argentines fired at the planes with everything they had; anti-aircraft guns, rockets, even with small arms fire. On the hills behind the town gun emplacements belched and hiccuped shells and tracer bullets, and we could see figures moving about as new guns were brought into position. The Harriers were striking at the damaged airport, and the bombs were exploding repeatedly.

Later that day the Argentines sent planes out to attack the Task Force. We heard the BBC reports that the Airport had been put out of action by the early morning bombing; we had no way of knowing how far that was true, as the Airport was now out of bounds to civilians. But some planes were taking off; a trickle of planes continued to do so throughout the rest of the conflict.

As I was going into the hospital later to visit some of the patients, the rocket launcher which the Argentines had located nearby leapt into life. I had not noticed any British planes approaching at that particular moment, but straining my eyes I saw two Harriers flying high overhead. I watched as the glowing candle streaked into the blue sky. It was a poor shot; the missile was some way behind the British planes when it exploded. The aircraft carried on unharmed and were soon out of sight. At one point in the combat that day we watched as the Argentine guns accidentally shot down one of their own planes. What was so tragic was the ecstasy of the watching soldiers and Argentine civilians, who at first believed that they had shot down a British Harrier. Until they realised what had actually happened, they danced and cheered, hugging each other joyfully, only to find out that in reality the loss was theirs.

I went on my way to comfort the patients, who were greatly alarmed by the outbreak of firing. I reflected angrily, as I had done several times before, on the callousness of people who placed military strategic defences close to hospitals. The football ground was not only a helicopter landing strip, but also by now a sizeable arsenal, as weapons and other equipment had accumulated round the perimeter. Sooner or later, I thought to myself, there is going to be an attack on this place. I hoped that by then the patients would have been properly evacuated to safety.

For most of the invasion, we civilians felt ourselves to be in little danger from the British attacks. On May 1 there was no bombing of the town by the British, even though there were numerous defensive gun stations close to the houses. All the bombing was concentrated on the Airport, some miles out of town. The aim of the exercise was to cripple the Airport and enforce the Exclusion Zone over air space as well as sea.

We had great trust in the British planes. Discussing the fighting one evening, I heard one of the Islanders say: 'If the British bomb me, I don't want to live.' I understood what he meant. We knew that our safety as civilians was important to the British soldiers who were planning our liberation.

However, we had to face the fact that with the escalation of the conflict and its extension on to the East Falkland mainland, our situation in the town was bound to change. An announcement by the Argentines did little to encourage us; they said that they would not be defending Port Stanley as a township but instead would be concentrating their defence on the strategic areas in and around it. Previously scornful of the capabilities of the British Task Force, they were now, in the aftermath of South Georgia, talking about the fierce fighting that was about to begin. The attempts to woo the residents with talk of creature comforts and a life full of opportunity and satisfaction under Argentine rule, stopped.

The attitude of the soldiers in the streets was

changing too. The blackout and curfew regulations had pitchforked us into a war situation, and the young men of the Argentine army were responding to this development by becoming hyper-cautious about moving in the dark, looking out for booby traps and ambushes. They were increasingly nervous. Minor incidents upset them, and they were suddenly trigger-happy. On several occasions homes were shot up because a patrol thought there was something or somebody in the house. As many of the houses are of timber construction, this was especially worrying. On one occasion Monsignor Spraggon counted twenty-eight bullet holes in his house walls. These were fired by the guards positioned immediately behind my house.

Iris and I moved our bed into a corridor in the Deanery which was safer than the bedroom. and built our own defensive walls with obsolete cast iron radiators.

The news of the retaking of South Georgia had lifted our morale considerbly. It was the first concrete evidence that the Task Force had arrived. The news that one of the occupied territories had been retaken was extremely exciting, and we began to think in terms of an end to the conflict, and to look forward to our own liberation.

The events of May 1 lifted our morale even higher. It was the first air attack on Stanley. It marked the beginning of the Royal Navy's operations off the Falklands. Whatever might be the situation in Port Stanley and whatever the dangers we might have to face, we were moving towards a critical phase.

The fighting continued through the day. In the evening at six o'clock, the Task Force opened fire on the coastlands with a massive bombardment. Argentine Mirage fighters attempted to intercept the Harriers, but we heard later that the only damage to the British planes was a small bullet hole in the tail of one of them. It was on that day that Brian Hanrahan, a BBC war correspondent reporting from the *Hermes*, coined a phrase that became famous overnight: 'I'm not allowed to say how many planes joined the raid . . . but I counted them all out and I counted them all back.'

The next day there was new confidence among the people of Port Stanley. It was impossible to ascertain what casualties the Argentines had suffered, but we knew that there had been losses, and that an attack on the small airstrip at Goose Green had also been successful. We did not rejoice over the fact that Argentine lives had been lost. But we were encouragd that now that the war had begun in earnest, the British had achieved significant results.

During that day, Captain Hussey called at the Monsignor's house to apologise for the accusations made the day before. It was quite a surprising development, but we were still extremely worried. In addition to the Haines family ex-members of the Falkland Defence Force still in Port Stanley – and also a number of other people involved in the administration of the Islands before the invasion – had also been arrested without warning and taken away.

But all in all, it was encouraging to witness the British forces in action, especially as we had been subjected to propaganda from the Argentines, who claimed that carriers had been sunk, that Prince Andrew had been killed, and that Admiral Woodward, faced with a hopeless task and the prospect of a disgraceful defeat, had committed suicide.

Early in the occupation I had been talking to an

Argentine official in the Upland Goose. 'One of the first casualties of war,' he assured me, 'is truth.' He was using one of the most overworked quotations in the Falklands War – it livened up many a routine dispatch in the newspapers. It was nevertheless entirely applicable to the Argentines. However much one tried to forget their stories, and however much one discounted them as propaganda, they still affected us. They made us laugh.

Had we known what lay in store for the men of both sides over the next few weeks, we might have found our encouragement somewhat premature. But we did not know, and it was better so.

10: Tragedies and triumphs

> . . . We tried to fight the damage. My
> impression was of immense calm, common
> sense and careful thinking by really every
> member of the ship's company.
>
> *Captain Sam Salt, speaking after the loss of
> the 'Sheffield'.*

On 2 May, the day after the bombing of the Airport,
the first major loss of life of the war occurred. It was
suffered by the Argentines, when the cruiser *General
Belgrano* was torpedoed by a British submarine and
over 300 on board died.

There have been numerous discussions as to the
exact purpose of the *Belgrano*'s voyage, the direction
she was heading in and the nature of her intentions
toward the Task Force. In Port Stanley, we certainly
were in no position to judge. My reaction, and that of
many others, was one of overwhelming sorrow. We
did not judge either side, but grieved at the loss of so
many young lives. We did not change our minds
about the necessity of finishing the conflict as quickly
as possible. We knew that would mean deaths. But
now those deaths had been made real to us in a single
horrifying statistic.

Two days later the Argentines fired the first of their Exocet missiles at HMS *Sheffield*. The ship was lost and twenty British men died. Although the numbers were much fewer than the *Belgrano*, it was impossible to draw much consolation from that fact. The Exocet, a surface-skimming missile with a range of over thirty miles and a devastating destructive capability, heralded a new phase of the war. The two sides were now engaged in warfare of a type not seen before in the world, using weapons that had not been fired in anger before. We knew that the results might be devastating.

The Argentine troops seemed to be getting a carefully edited version of events. They were only now being told that there had been action at South Georgia, but it appeared that they had not been told that the Dependency had been retaken. Nevertheless, the loss of the *Belgrano*, which caused scenes of mass grief in Buenos Aires, could not be kept from the troops on the Islands.

The atmosphere hardened. Houses were searched repeatedly and anything remotely usable as a weapon was confiscated. Buildings were checked without warning. The West Store was searched several times. It was a 'safe house', where a large number of people were spending the curfew hours each night. On one occasion the Store was checked twice in a single night, the occupants being forced to line up in the street, facing the wall with their hands in the air. Some of them were elderly, and the night was very cold.

An issue of identity cards for civilians was begun. A census was taken of vehicles in Port Stanley, and many of these were soon commandeered. A special search was made for illegal transmitters. People began to dread the knock at the door at night which could mean the arrival of the soldiers or police.

As the situation deteriorated I continued to do what I could. Morale became crucial. Rumours continued to circulate. People's minds were stretched taut, under constant strain, and some were ready to believe any horror story that was circulating.

Not all problems were quickly resolved. On the day of the bombing of the Airport, I had been to the Cathedral. I found that the vestry lock had been forced. The church had not been broken into, but the forced door had given access to the belfry. The altar rail had ben renched off to force the vestry door, and all the fuses had been removed.

I managed to repair the damage quite quickly, and from that moment on, I made sure that the church was always locked when not in use.

Some time later, I had a telephone message to say that Argentine soldiers had been digging holes in the cemetery. I immediately phoned the Monsignor to tell him what I was doing, and went up to the cemetery where the person who had phoned me was waiting. Remonstrating with the soldiers had no effect. They pointed out that they were only able to act on the orders of their superior officer, and that I therefore ought to go and see their superior officer personally. I drove off with my informant to act as translator, and we found the officer.

'Your men are digging trenches in the cemetery,' I said. 'Please tell them to stop.'

The lieutenant looked at me uncomprehendingly. 'Why?' he asked.

'For many reasons,' I argued. 'It is quite likely that they will uncover some human remains. That is perfectly possible. But more than that, it is consecrated ground. Your men should leave it immediately.'

127

The officer looked long and hard at the ground, as if some arrangement of grass and dust at his feet was of much greater importance than our protest.

'This will offend the people,' I added.

The lieutenant raised his head and looked at us superciliously without speaking for a moment. Then he said to me, 'Can I put some men in the church tower?'

I was taken aback by the suggestion.

'You have a very high church tower,' he remarked. 'Can I put men there?'

'No,' I said sharply.

'Why not?'

'Because the church is a place of refuge,' I retorted, 'and there is no place there for armed men.'

'Look-outs,' he suggested mildly. 'Not armed.'

'No,' I insisted.

He sighed. 'We will stop the digging,' he said. Two military police arrived at that moment, summoned by the Monsignor when he got my message. So the digging came to a stop, and the tower remained secure.

A few days after that, I had a visit from Blumer-Reve who had come to apologise for the church break-in. The excuse was that some troops had forced the door because they thought they saw someone in the belfry. All I could think at the time was that they had taken a very odd route to get to the belfry.

The excavations of the troops came much nearer home. They dug on every street corner and in many of the gardens. I was told on one occasion that they were digging up my garden.

'Aren't you going to stop them?' demanded Iris.

I raised my eyebrows. 'Stop them? Why?'

'Well, look at them!'

I watched the Argentine soldiers in our hen run.

They were digging away industriously. I had been told that the troops were in our garden and I had hurried back home to find them clearing a patch of scrub. It looked as though they were preparing a defensive position.

'Yes,' I said thoughtfully. 'I'll have to put in an official protest about this.'

I looked again at the efforts of the soldiers. They were making quite good progress. For the past few months I had been intending to clear that patch myself, but had never had time. I grinned at Iris.

'On the other hand,' I added, 'I think I'll wait just a little while before I complain. I'll let them finish the job first . . .'

The sinking of the ships brought home to us the reality of death in battle, and it was not only the sailors who died. On May 4 a British pilot, Nicholas Taylor, was shot down and killed in a raid on Goose Green. He was the first Harrier pilot to die. I was told to be ready to go to officiate at his funeral, but heard nothing more until several days later, when I learned that he had been buried at Darwin with a military funeral. Two days after the death of Lieutenant Taylor, two aircraft were lost by accident. We mourned each of these deaths. We did not only grieve for British lives. The sadness of war was fast becoming a reality, and we saw it in the faces of scared Argentine soldiers as much as in the grim statistics of casualties that we received. It strengthened our hope that the matter would be soon resolved.

On May 9 the British began a sea and air bombardment. From that date my diary is a list of military actions observed and heard. Three separate attacks on Monday 10 May; naval action on the Tuesday; Argentine plane losses on the Wednesday; on Friday 14 May the noise of explosions was so loud that I could not hear the greetings on the radio.

On Saturday 15 May, a 45-man detachment from D Squadron, acting on information supplied by an eight-man SAS team that had been scouting the Pebble Island area, landed on West Falkland and in a brilliant operation destroyed eleven Argentine aircraft and withdrew in a force 9 gale. The operation was supported by naval bombardment from nearby frigates. The British, who were heavily outnumbered, had no casualties. The effect on the morale of the troops must have been tremendous. Its effect on us, when news came through to Port Stanley, was equally heartening. This group of Islands, garrisoned by thousands of Argentine troops, was still able to be attacked successfully by a handful of men. The British were not only coming. They had arrived. They had set foot on Falklands soil. We knew our turn would not be long delayed.

We were excited; but we knew, too, that there was danger. The constant bombardment of Port Stanley was a reminder to us that around the town, in other places on the Islands, and out at sea men were dying. From ten o'clock at night to two in the morning, the salvoes of shells exploded around Stanley. In a strange way, however, it was comforting. They were shells fired by our people, help was at hand, and we were not the targets. The disturbed sleep was not a problem. I found myself being disappointed if we had a quiet night.

The attack on Pebble Island, which was followed by increased bombing, had a predictable effect on the morale of the Argentine troops stationed in Stanley. Their officers seemed to be finding it difficult to keep control; the earlier insistence that the soldiers should have respect for private property and the rights of civilians was sometimes less than rigorously maintained. I was concerned at the danger to empty houses, especially when the Argentines began to order compulsory evacuation in certain areas which were at risk. Power cuts had threatened the contents of the owners' freezers, and I had promised a number of people to keep an eye on things. Now it was obvious that vandalism and looting was happening.

It seemed in the beginning that the culprits were only searching for food, because the first instances of looting only involved thefts from freezers and food-stores. Then valuables began disappearing. When you have to leave home suddenly you make sure that the doors and windows are locked, but you don't always hide valuables or personal treasures away. Some things were being stolen.

The authorities tried to keep their soldiers under control. Mrs Stacey, the old lady who was spending curfew hours in her nephew's home, had her own house broken into twice on successive nights. The Argentine military police asked permission to station a man in the house after that. But their efforts were only partly successful. Break-ins continued in various parts of the town, and though a few arrests were made the situation continued to get worse.

131

11: The beginning of the end

> Since Britain moved to recapture the
> Falklands, the Navy has fired a thousand
> salvoes, making this the most intense
> period of British bombardment since the
> Second World War.
>
> *Brian Hanrahan reporting 16 May.*

I stood at the Deanery door and watched a troop carrier rumble past. The soldiers looked tired, as well they might; it had been a heavy bombardment the previous night, and few of us had slept. As they passed the Cathedral, as if by an unspoken word of command, they crossed themselves.

It was Thursday 20 May. I was leaving to go to Government House, and my blood was up.

Disturbing news had reached me and the Monsignor that since the bombing raids of May 1 on Port Stanley Airport and that of Goose Green, the civilians of Goose Green (which is the largest farm settlement in the Falklands) had been imprisoned by the Argentines in the club hall. The news came through by the 'diddle-dee telegraph', that unique word of mouth which operates among our community in the

Islands, on Wednesday 19 May – a day otherwise only marked by a lunchtime power-cut and a greeting to Iris and myself from our family on the BBC radio programme *Calling the Falklands*. Instinctively, we knew this was not a panic rumour. The diddle-dee telegraph is reliable.

We had made an immediate and very strong complaint to Blumer-Reve and demanded that immediate action be taken to ascertain the truth or otherwise of the story. The result of our complaint was a summons at 9 a.m. the next day to Government House to see General Menendez. And that was where I was going.

Monsignor and I repeated what we had heard, and asked for his comments. Menendez stared at us thoughtfully.

'The people you are talking about are not imprisoned. By their own request, they are living together in one building. They say that it makes them feel more secure.' He shaped his words carefully. 'If they so wished they could leave that building at any time.'

We disputed this. 'We request that we be allowed to make a personal visit to Goose Green,' we stated. 'We wish to see the people themselves, to assure ourselves that they are well. Also such a visit by us would be an encouragement to the families of those people, who are at present living in Port Stanley. They will know that their relatives are in good health and are being looked after.'

Menendez shrugged. 'That is not permissible.'

'We do not believe that these people are not being held against their will,' I said. 'We know these people well. Our information is that they –'

'I will explain,' interrupted Menendez. He narrowed his eyes. 'One of my officers acted improperly.

He was angered by the death of men under his command when on May 1 the British bombed Goose Green. He locked up the people because he believed that they had been in communication with the enemy.'

A glance passed between myself and Monsignor Spraggon. This was a change of tune. Menendez continued smoothly, 'It was a wise act; there was much resentment against your people. Naturally I expected that the prisoners would be released in a few days. Their continued imprisonment is without my authority and against my wishes. I have already sent instructions that they are to be released. These instructions have not been carried out.'

He frowned, as if to convey the exasperation of finding such disobedience in the ranks. The flow of his precise, careful words continued. 'I shall now instruct my personal assistant to go to Goose Green, secure the safety of the civilians, and report to me personally that this has been done.'

Menendez paused impressively. I repeated my request. 'I wish to go to Goose Green myself.'

'That is not permissible,' the General said flatly. 'My assistant will do what is necessary. Of course,' he added casually, 'helicopter transport is not always readily available in circumstances such as these . . . he may not be able to make the journey immediately. It may be that he has to wait some time.'

We pressed him for details. When would he be able to arrange for their release? What guarantees had we that such incidents would not be repeated?

Menendez fielded our questions gracefully, and over the course of the ensuing discussion – which was a lengthy one – altered the story again. Finally he gave us his personal assurance that the imprisonment would be ended, and with that we had to be content. It turned out to be an empty promise – the Argentines never did release their prisoners at Goose Green, and they were freed eventually by the British ten days later.

Such episodes fuelled the frustrations that could not be altogether controlled. We had had much encouragement; first the embarkation and arrival of the Task Force, then the bombing of the Airport, and the landing at Pebble Island. But it was also very hard to know that our troops were here – had even set foot on the Islands – and had withdrawn. We knew the reasons, we trusted the generals. We knew that the weather would not hold out, and that a landing must be made soon if at all. It was the waiting which was hard.

Some of the resentment was directed at those of us who were exposed in situations of leadership. I was talking with some people at the Upland Goose one night, and it was said by one lady that the people were panicking. I disagreed; my daily travelling about Stanley didn't bear it out. At this the speaker began to criticise me, accusing me of being an outsider and unable to know how the people felt. But I was able to counter that my judgement was based on talking with fifty people or more every day; at the hospital, in the stores, on the streets, in their homes; so I could claim to have a good knowledge of the way the residents were reacting to the situation.

But it was not very long before the event we had looked for and prayed for took place. On Friday 21 May the British did make their landing, at a place which has become as well-known as Port Stanley itself: San Carlos Bay.

12: San Carlos and after

Ships pass to embarked forces.
1. D-Day 21 May 82
2. H-Hour is 210639Z May 1982
3. Break down and issue first line
ammunition forthwith
4. Act immediately.

*British field orders issued prior to Port San
Carlos landing.*

I am not writing a military history of the Falklands
War. Others have done the job far better than I could,
confined to Port Stanley as I was and with limited
access to news. Men who sailed with the fleet and
marched with the men have written their accounts, and
I have no experiences of the battlefields to add to theirs.

For those of us living in Port Stanley, life became
simultaneously exhilarating and alarming. We re-
joiced at the landing at Port San Carlos, but grieved at
the loss of lives and ships that followed. The roll of
ships that went down was a roll of lives lost; the
Sheffield, the *Ardent*, the *Antelope*, the *Coventry*, the
Atlantic Conveyor. The news from abroad was no less
comforting. The impetus for the military operation

was largely the failure of peace talks. There seemed little sign of a last-minute negotiated settlement. There was going to be a final battle. It would be a hard-fought one. By now the soldiers had dug themselves in permanently into our vegetable garden; the gun emplacements were moving nearer to civilian houses. We prayed a great deal as we watched and waited. And still the Lord bore Iris and me up with his strength and comfort. I still had the wonderful sense of safety, the conviction that I would come through alive, and with this confidence I was able to go about my visiting and do my work even when there was firing and bombardment.

May 28 dawned with a very heavy barrage on Port Stanley. At the same time, though we did not know it until later, the British troops were advancing from the already-liberated San Carlos and Port San Carlos to Goose Green and Darwin. In a bitter battle, the Paras' CO, Colonel 'H' Jones, was killed during a gallant assault on a machine-gun position. By the end of the day I was able to write in my diary, 'Goose Green and Darwin captured by Paras.'

The effect on our morale was tremendous. The Argentines, who had seized the entire Falkland Islands, had now lost possession of vital strategic sites. More than that, the people who four weeks ago had been locked in the club hall at Goose Green would sleep that night in their own beds and under British protection. It was wonderful news.

The curfew hours were further increased. We were ordered off the streets at 4 p.m. On Sunday 30 May I cancelled Evensong. There was a great deal of noise from the direction of the Airport that night, and some bombing was audible.

The week following was the preparation for the

attack on Bluff Cove, or, more precisely, Fitzroy. It took place against a background of renewed diplomatic activity in the West as a way was sought for the avoidance of the battle for Port Stanley which was now only days away. As at Port San Carlos, military success was followed by retaliation from the defending Argentines, and the *Galahad* and the *Tristram* were severely damaged.

After the news of the attack on Fitzroy we were greatly disturbed. Bits and pieces of information filtered through and we realised that there had been a major attack with British casualties; not having detailed information, we feared the worst. When we did find out that fifty people had died, although the number was much less than we had feared it was little consolation. There was great distress among the Islanders that so many people had lost their lives.

But the tragedy really marked the hastening of the end. Military actions increased on the route to Port Stanley as the British advance gathered strength. By June 11 the word 'yomping' had featured in every British newspaper's headlines as the troops pushed across virtually impossible terrain at an incredible pace, and the troops were at our gates.

If you were to study the lie of the land on that approach, you might well wonder how it was that the Argentines ever lost the battle. It is low ground, interrupted by high rocky outcrops along which the Argentine troops were dug in. The defenders had positions in ideal high ground cover. Logically the British ought to have been decimated. But it says a great deal for the ability and the strategy of our armed forces that the losses were much fewer than might have been expected.

The British paratroops took up positions on and around Mount Longdon; the Marines and other troops were moving up from Fitzroy to Tumbledown, and a further advance was being made up to Sapper Hill, along the coastal ground. This three-pronged attack was a classic 'pincer' operation, and by the time it was established the Argentines would be trapped in Port Stanley, their defences forming a half circle against the surrounding forces; at their backs was the sea.

On the morning of 11 June, Iris and I made the short journey from the Upland Goose Hotel to our home, as we had done every morning since we had begun to spend the curfew hours in the Hotel, as several others in our neighbourhood were doing. It was 8.30 a.m. There were soldiers on the harbour front, drilling and practising weapon handling. They paid little attention to us. Many of them appeared to be having difficulty, as if the weapons they were handling were unfamiliar. In the West the bombardment was continuing. As we went inside the house, the building shook. We almost didn't notice it; explosions were part of our lives. 'Another hit on the Airport,' I remarked to Iris. An hour later we discovered that the noise had been a direct hit on the Police Station next door.

The bombardment was, in a way, not a source of fear to us. We had prayed together before leaving the hotel, and we had asked for strength to face whatever might happen that day. We knew God would give it to us. We also had great confidence in the British forces' reluctance to fire on civilian homes, and the bombardment was concentrated on the open areas around the town. But the initial excitement we had felt over the shelling, the surge of expectation at each *whoosh* and *crunch*, had given way to a constant sorrow at the deaths and woundings that were happening. It had been a long catalogue of grief that had brought us to this point – necesary, but no less grievous. The *Belgrano*, the loss of *Sheffield* and other ships, and the horror of *Sir Galahad* and *Sir Tristram* that very week, had brought home to us the reality of war and the suffering it brings with it. We had known that men would die and ships would sink. The knowledge that it had happened, and was happening, was a chilling reminder of the harsh truth that we were witnessing a life-and-death struggle. Also, I was disturbed by the prospect of fighting in the streets of Stanley; and my daily encounters with the people I was ministering to kept their suffering constantly in mind.

That evening, the sadness came very close to the heart of our community. It had been a day of heavy action. The airport had been bombed again; the Police Station next door had been hit, and numerous men were attempting to clear up the mess. During the day the Argentine hospital ship, the *Bahai Paraiso*, arrived in harbour and unloaded a large consignment of food for the troops. It was rumoured that weapons were being unloaded as well. The ship left harbour at four o'clock in the afternoon. The shelling beyond Moody Brook on Mount Longdon had become fiercer, and was getting nearer to the town. By evening, shells were landing in the harbour.

At around midnight, tragedy struck. A number of people were sleeping together in the house of John Fowler, the Education Superintendent, in Ross Road West. The Argentines were shelling Mount Longdon, and the British were returning fire. There was also a naval bombardment in progress. A shell fell not far beyond this house and exploded, and another exploded a little way in front of the house. Shrapnel from the second shell entered the house and injured a number of people, two of whom died immediately. The third, an elderly lady of 82, Mary Goodwin, was seriously wounded. She died a little time afterwards on the morning of the cease-fire. These three were the only residents of Port Stanley to die because of the invasion.

The next day, the whole community mourned. We felt the bereavement as if it had happened to our own families. Death, which had previously been raging on the hillsides, was now in our homes. Many were understandably frightened as well as shocked. I was sustained by the conviction which had been with me from the beginning, that I would come through alive; I had a quiet assurance that this was God's plan for me. But from that moment on, it was impossible to feel any thrill as our guns fired.

That day – Saturday 12 June – a sustained barrage was mounted against the Argentine forces. There seemed to be a shell fired every few seconds of the day. The noise was deafening. In the afternoon – it was a fine, sunny day – I walked out along Davies Street to visit friends. It was like walking through a ghost town, albeit one being shelled by a barrage of high explosive. The Argentine guns had been moved back from their exposed positions, where they could be easily knocked out, into the gardens of the houses on the south side of the street. The houses had been compulsorily evacuated a few days earlier. The occupants were now living wherever people had space to take them in. I had visited such homes many times in the past weeks; one would be shown through a kitchen where there seemed to be more chairs than usual around the table, and then it would be necessary to pick one's way over mattresses and sleeping bags in the hallway and all the rooms – in some houses as many as eighteen people were sleeping. It was like the London blitz, when people crammed into the Underground stations, and a similar camaraderie was built up as different families shared the same bedrooms and discovered resources of humour and friendliness that they might not otherwise have found. In one of those houses an old lady was confined to bed through injury, and remained cheerful each night as a variety of neighbours camped out on the floor around her bed.

Following the deaths in Ross Road West, another order was issued that day, requiring all persons living in the part of Stanley west of the Monument to find alternative accommodation by four o'clock that afternoon.

I counted the Argentine guns as they fired, until I reached the house. I stood in the garden with my friends and watched the shells landing on Mount Longdon, cratering the rough ground and raising enormous clouds of smoke.

'The Paras are up there,' said my friend soberly. We listened to the heavy smack of the shells landing. 'I hope they're well dug in.' We went indoors in some distress.

The fighting continued on through the night and into Sunday. I had time to scribble in my diary, 'Quiet night, apart from Arg. guns'. The next day was another day of fine weather. At lunchtime I found myself in Davies Street again; I had arranged to meet an elderly man there, and we were going to empty the freezer in a house which had been left empty when the occupants left for one of the farms. We had been jointly asked to keep an eye on the house and its contents. It had stood empty for ten weeks now, and strangely enough the Argentines had not interfered with it yet. We were thrilled by this, but now that electricity supplies were unreliable, it seemed that the best thing to do would be to empty the freezer and distribute the food amongst the neighbours, rather than see it go rotten when the electricity failed.

I was walking along Davies Street to carry out that errrand. The noise of the bombardment was deafening, and there was a constant spattering of fragments on the pavement. I bent down at one point to see what it was, and picked up a piece of metal. It was shrapnel, and it was still hot.

I fealt no fear, even though the shrapnel was falling all around. I felt very peaceful and under the Lord's protection. I walked on, and eventually reached the empty house. It was situated on an elevated part of the street, to reach which a number of steps had to be climbed. I came up on to the higher level and into a clearer view of the bombardment.

As I paused at the gate, looking round to see whether the man I had come to meet had arrived yet, there was a particularly thunderous increase in the noise of the attack. As it subsided I heard a woman's voice calling urgently.

'Padre! Padre!'

I looked round. It was Mrs Castle, a lady I knew well. She was leaning out of the window of a van. 'Don't go any further!' she called. Suddenly aware of the danger on that high ground, I ducked instinctively behind some bushes growing near the gate. Then I realised how incongruous that was – the bushes were useless cover against the stuff that was coming down. I smiled at myself and ran to the van.

'Get in,' said Mrs Castle. There was panic in her voice, and a great concern for my safety. 'Come on, let us take you back down into the lower street.'

I decided to call it a day, and got into the van. At that precise moment—it was 12 noon—there was a direct hit on a house about a hundred yards away. The house was gutted. It was the house from which the elderly man I had planned to meet had been evacuated a few days earlier.

The driver took us down to the lower level of the street. There was a flurry of activity in the surrounding houses. When the first house was hit, other families still living near Davies Street began evacuating their houses as well. People were carrying clothes and possessions into the street, heading for the houses of friends who lived further away from that area of Stanley.

The barrage that day was the final assault from behind Moody Brook and the capture of all the strategic high ground around the town. The troops were poised for the final attack. Port Stanley, with smouldering fires, buildings and demoralised soldiers, was ready for the taking.

I was becoming desperately tired. The noise of the ceaseless bombardment was wearing me and Iris down, and the events of that particular Sunday had been more exhausting than most. We went back to the Upland Goose as usual, and spent the evening chatting with the twenty or so other refugees and the residents of the Hotel. I suggested to Iris that we should sleep downstairs in the dining room that night, because that might be a little quieter than upstairs; so we brought our sleeping bags down and settled ourselves on the floor.

To my surprise I fell asleep immediately. The next thing I knew was that the telephone was ringing and somebody was banging on the front door. I opened my eyes and groped for my watch. It was six o'clock.

13: Liberation

> He has sent me to bring good news to the
> humble, to bind up the broken-hearted, to
> proclaim liberty to captives and release
> those in prison (Isaiah 61:1).

*Text for sermon of thanksgiving preached at
the Cathedral, Port Stanley, 20 June.*

An Argentine voice at the door was saying, 'The
British are not far away. They will be here in two
hours time.'

All thought of further sleep was out of the question.
We dressed, had a cup of tea and a wash, and waited
impatiently to see what would happen.

I received a telephone call asking me to go to the
Hospital as soon as possible. Mary Goodwin had died
that morning of her wounds, and though she was not a
member of my congregation but of St Mary's, I was
asked to go up to the hospital to discuss the possibility
of a joint funeral for all three deceased, in which both
churches would take part.

At 8.30 – the earliest I was allowed out under the
curfew rules – I left the Hotel. In the street outside
there were scores of soldiers who were leaving the

Town Hall. They had been sheltering there during the night. It was a sharp, frosty morning, and they were complaining bitterly about having to be outdoors. As I went to the Hospital I was amazed at the numbers of soldiers who were falling back to the Hospital area. There was a general retreat going on.

Overnight it was like bonfire night. Tracer bullets and shells were passing in both directions, and heavy shelling was coming from Wireless Ridge across the harbour. As the crescendo of noise increased, there were hundreds of soldiers milling around the Hospital, some of them – judging by their Red Cross armbands – having left the Hostel which had been previously taken over by the Argentines and used as a military hospital.

I made my way through the troops and entered the Hospital. It was a great joy to be able to comfort the patients who were there and to be able to say to them, 'I know it's noisy, and I know it's frightening – but please wait just a little longer. This is your last day under Argentine rule.' I was able to go around and tell each little group the same thing. At first they couldn't believe it. Most were elderly patients, and were sitting together in the safer places in the Hospital away from flying glass. In the X-ray room, where some patients had been placed, I sat holding an old lady's hands, talking softly to her.

'Bear it a little longer . . . just a few hours. Just a few hours longer, then it will all be over.' But the invasion had lasted ten weeks, and the thought that it would be over in two hours was too much for many of the patients to take in. Those who could were overjoyed, and so were some of the staff who had not yet had full details of the night's events.

We discussed the funeral arrangements – which had to be abandoned and re-thought, as things turned out. The undertaker was at the Hospital by then, and we said the things that had to be said, and then it was time to leave. But the Argentine authorities refused to allow us to leave, saying it was too dangerous. 'You must wait until an escort is available,' we were told. Shortly afterwards an Argentine policeman came and escorted the undertaker and me away. I went back to the Upland Goose and then home. Outside our home the troops were streaming past from west to east right through the town. Looking back towards the Hospital area we saw that a fire had started. Smoke was rising over the area I had just left.

It was by then about ten o'clock. Questions were running through our minds. Were the troops in general retreat, or were they merely falling back to a new defensive line within Port Stanley? If that were so, then we would see the final battle all too closely, because it would take place in the crowded streets of our town. And when would the British arrive? Would it still be a matter of hours, or were they close by now?

The morning merged into a blur. My recollection is hazy; the hours were racing by. For much of the time Iris and I lost contact with each other; I was at the Hospital and elsewhere, and we were both in the Upland Goose as much as in our own home, and we missed each other several times. A number of families also had been told to evacuate their houses that morning, and Iris had been wlcoming them to their new accommodation. All I can remember clearly is that tide of troops streaming past, and the sight of several of the Argentine Padres thrusting rosaries into the hands of some of the soldiers as they passed.

By lunchtime there were white flags flying over

Port Stanley, and things had quietened down. I went out on the street again.

Coming along Ross Road like a giant Colossus, swinging a large walking stick, was a man wearing combat uniform. I thought he must be a general at the very least, so imposing did he seem as he strode into Port Stanley. In fact he was a British journalist, Max Hastings, who had been with No. 2 Paras on their final assault on Port Stanley. When later I saw him in the Upland Goose he was standing by the bar surrounded by people. I learned from him that the British troops had been stopped just past the Monument, half a mile away. Negotiations were taking place for a cease-fire. He said he was going back there, and I went with him to the Monument where the British lines were. On the way I saw the bodies of two dead Argentines lying in the road, and wondered whether they were perhaps the last two people to die in the conflict.

There were some light tanks drawn up on the road, and a large number of Paras. I greeted many of them, and they asked where they could get water, which was in short supply. I was greeted by friendly cries on all sides, and some, seeing my clerical collar, greeted me appropriately—one man said sincerely, 'Padre, I've prayed so much during these past few weeks—I'm going to be a real church man from now on . . .' There were similar comments from many of the Paras, spoken half seriously and with a grin, and in many cases I am sure that the sentiments were quite genuine.

I met the army Padre, Derek Heaver, and we spent a few minutes together. And then I went back to Stanley, to home and Iris. About half an hour later, I went outside again. The troops were moving again, but now in the opposite direction. I could not understand why. And even in the middle of the crush of bodies, a voice called my name. It was the young Argentine who had worshipped at the Cathedral, the one who had been a servant at Menendez' office.

'What is happening?' I called back to him.

'There has been a cease-fire agreed,' he said. 'We have to move back into town until four o'clock. That is when General Menendez meets your officers to negotiate.'

He disappeared as his colleagues bore him past in the crowd. But he had told me the news I wanted most of all to hear. There was a cease-fire. It was over. The occupation was at an end.

That night we all slept in our own beds. Iris and I thought that was wonderful, but we had hardly settled back into normality and a good sleep when there was an enormous banging and crackling twenty-five yards from the back of the Deanery. The nearby squash-court was on fire. It was believed that the Argentines had been using the building as an ammunition store: so within minutes we were all evacuated again. It seemed like the last straw, when we had only just arrived back home! However, it turned out to be a false alarm, the fire was brought under control, and it was found that there was no ammunition dump there. Apparently asbestos, of which the building was largely constructed, makes a noise very like exploding ammunition when it burns, and that was what had caused the scare. It was not the only fire that night, and because we had limited fire-fighting resources, fire became a new threat and continued to be so for some time.

The next day I spent some of the time re-erecting the flagpole I had dismantled when the Argentines invaded. Soon the Union Jack was flying over the Deanery again.

Towards lunchtime, I saw a string of vehicles parked outside the Globe Hotel. I decided to investigate. The atmosphere inside the Hotel was festive; the celebrations were in full swing. I was pressed to join the merrymaking, but I was more interested at that time in finding out as much as I could about what was happening. Eventually one of the drivers told me he was taking his vehicle out along the Airport road.

'Mind if I come along?' I asked.

'Jump in,' he said cheerfully. So I sat in the back with one or two soldiers, and we were taken to the place where the Juliet Company of the Marines were disarming Argentine troops. It was signficant that Juliet Company were doing this, because they were the old NP8901 company which had been in the Islands on April 1st and had been captured by the Argentines. I had not known that they were there, until one of them greeted me.

'The OC's here, Padre,' he told me. I did not recognise the Major at first. He was well wrapped up against the bitter wind that was blowing. I greeted him, and we had a brief conversation. When I turned from speaking to him, a group of four or five Marines in very high spirits were waiting to say hello. They were the Marines I had last seen in military detention, when Monsignor and I had been allowed to visit them after they had surrendered to the Argentines several days after the invasion. Then I had been allowed ten minutes with five imprisoned men: now we were meeting in freedom. It was an emotional meeting for us all.

There were greetings, and there were departures. A

short time after the hostilities had ceased, I was leaving the Deanery to go into town. As I opened my front gate two men walked past from the direction of the Upland Goose: I recognised Blumer-Reve and Captain Hussey. When they saw me they put down their heavy cases gratefully, and we chatted for a few minutes. It was a time for goodbyes, and glad though I was to see the back of the Argentine occupying forces, I did not want to part discourteously from Blumer-Reve, who had been my main point of access to the temporary governing powers, or Hussey, with whom I had had a cordial relationship, given the circumstances. I smiled at a memory of a conversation I had had with Captain Hussey several weeks earlier. He was a keen jogger – the only Argentine I ever saw exercising – and I often saw him in his tracksuit on Ross Road. During the final approach of the British I had asked him jokingly if he had begun packing. 'I have nothing to pack,' he retorted. 'Not even your tracksuit?' I countered, and we both had laughed. Now it seemed that the Captain had had a great deal to pack after all.

'Where are you heading for?' I asked.

They nodded towards the helicopter departure point, some distance away. I indicated my Landrover parked nearby.

'Why don't you put your baggage in my vehicle?' I suggested. 'Those things look heavy. I can take you there in two minutes.'

They smiled regretfully and shook their heads. Blumer-Reve looked past me at the garden and smiled. 'I see you have your flag flying again,' he remarked. We contemplated the red, white and blue fabric snapping in the light breeze. 'And your flagpole restored too,' he observed. I grinned back. He smiled civilly. 'I expect that things are now as you have desired them, Padre Bagnall.'

They reached for their cases. I watched as they hoisted them off the ground. The bags looked very heavy. 'Can't I give you a lift?' I asked again.

Blumer-Reve looked back at me with an expression which might have been either self-respect or consideration for me. 'No,' he said quietly. 'This is the way things must be.'

They strode down the road, and that was the last I saw of either of them.

The Argentine troops were allowed a certain amount of freedom of movement, once they had been disarmed. Sometimes their frustration and disappointment exploded into incidents. My first encounter with the problem came when I answered a knock at the door to find some soldiers asking whether we had any brooms, pails or mops to spare.

'It's to clean the Post Office,' they explained. We found some cleaning materials. It seemed an odd time to do spring-cleaning, but the soldiers did not offer any further explanation. Later that day I found out that the previous night Argentine soldiers had broken into the Post Office during the night and created havoc, overturning tables and cupboards and scattering the incoming mail everywhere. They had smeared the room and its contents with their own excrement. In the cleaning-up that followed quantities of mail had to be destroyed. Most of it had been destined for the Argentine troops serving on the Islands.

With the cease-fire, my role changed. Whatever leadership I had been required to give during the occupation was no longer required. The structures of

Port Stanley social life began to reinstate themselves very quickly, as people returned from the Camp, including some of the elected civic leaders and town officers, and the normal pattern of life began to reassert itself. However, though I was (quite properly) no longer considered as a spokesman of the community, there was still a tremendous amount to do. I continued my pastoral work, and normal Cathedral services.

I felt it very important that there should be a Thanksgiving Service for our deliverance, at the Cathedral. I approached General Moore about this. I wrote him a letter, putting forward the suggestion, and then decided to deliver it personally to make sure it got to him. I set out for Government House, which the British were using as their headquarters. I had just visited the building in order to speak to the Argentine authorities. Now the situation was reversed, and the British were once again in Government House.

I was shown into a room in which there were two or three officers. I spoke to one of them.

'I'd like to speak to General Moore, please.'

A lean, pleasant-faced man turned round and replied: 'I'm General Moore.' By his manner he put me completely at ease. He reached for the letter I was holding and read it through there and then. After a brief discussion the date of the Thanksgiving Service was set for the following Sunday.

The task of returning Port Stanley to normal life involved hard work, and we were grateful to the troops, who now worked on restoring essential services as speedily as possible. The water mains had been shattered, and in the last few days of fighting the electricity cables had been brought down. Everything had to be meticulously checked in case the Argentines had left booby-traps. The Airport had suffered heavy attacks throughout the final campaign, and much work was being done to repair the damage and get traffic moving again. In addition, the numerous mines scattered around the town were a serious problem; the Argentine prisoners could only give limited information as to the location of minefields, because many of those laying the mines kept no records or were not following instructions properly.

The problem of accommodating the British soldiers was solved by billeting many of them in the town — twelve officers and three other soldiers stayed with us in the Deanery. The Argentine troops were moved out to temporary accommodation at the Airfield while the necessary diplomatic procedures were performed to permit their return to Argentina. Within a very short time, the soldiers who had taken part in the liberation were either gone or preparing to leave, and new troops were shortly arriving to garrison the Island and help in the unglamorous work of tidying up. I had thought that General Moore's choice of the 20th for the Thanksgiving Service had been rather an early date, but I quickly realised that he had had in mind the fact that the forces were to be leaving the Islands as soon as possible.

The Thanksgiving Service was one of the great experiences of my life. There were other Thanksgiving Services held — for instance each of the Para units held their own service — I conducted two or three services for individual units. But the service of June 20th was special. Because the church was so small, there was room only for representatives of the military units and the civilians. Even so, the church was packed: 400 people crammed into a building designed to hold a maximum of 250. I picked my way carefully to the pulpit to avoid treading on anyone. While I was speaking somebody was standing inches away pointing a microphone at me, and space was so cramped I accidentally punched it several times as I gestured to make a point. The atmosphere was deeply moving.

I preached from Isaiah 61:1. I began by looking back to that other Sunday, Palm Sunday, when I had gazed down at a similarly packed church from the same pulpit and had found it difficult to hold back my tears. Now I felt emotion again, but this time the emotion was joyfulness. I looked down at the rows of uniformed men, many of them still obviously exhausted by the long and gruelling military operation. 'Do you feel the sense of release which is ours? The people of the Island,' I assured them, 'welcome you with open arms.'

A few days later I was chatting to a Guards Officer who had been at the Thanksgiving Service.

'I was sitting on the floor,' he told me, 'just under the pulpit. You know, that text, the sermon, the service – made it all worth while for me. It made sense of what's happened, despite the men we lost and all the sorrow.'

The Falklands are a different place now, different in scores of ways. For one thing, people know where we are. There is talk of development, of finance and tourism. One hindrance might be the minefields, which the Argentines left largely unmapped. Whole areas we used to walk in and enjoy are barred to us for years ahead. We have been issued with minefield maps, on which large areas around Port Stanley have been heavily overscored in red, indicating danger. It will probably never be possible to clear them all, and some places will be permanently closed to the public. For Iris and myself this has meant one immediate change in our normal routine; my peat bog is in one of the prohibited areas, and I have had to make other arrangements to get fuel for the winter.

Of course, a major change in Port Stanley is the change from a quiet Island town to a major strategic garrison. We are used to the sight of British soldiers in our midst now. After the departure of the men who had taken part in the recapture of the Islands, others arrived to begin the task of maintaining a military presence and helping civilian life back to a more normal pattern. I was very grateful to the men who appeared one day to restore my vegetable garden to order; the Argentines, when they abandoned the defensive position they had established there, had dumped wrecked equipment in trenches and turned large parts of my garden into a sea of mud and litter. Several cheerful soldiers soon had it cleared.

Our opportunities for ministry have vastly increased. Many of the troops have little to do on their evenings off, and we have started a coffee-bar in the Deanery to which a number of them come. Iris's home-made biscuits have proved very popular. We also had some troops billeted with us in the Deanery, as had most other families, as the need to house troops was urgent – the weather deteriorated very quickly in the final days of the occupation.

As an honorary Missions to Seamen Chaplain and also an Officiating Chaplain RN to add to my normal parish work, there is much to do. We have had opportunities to share the gospel with many of these men, and in their turn they have helped and supported us in many practical ways.

Our congregations at the Cathedral are increased by servicemen who attend. One of them plays the organ for us. We have been praying for years for an additional organist, but little thought to get one in this way. In fact we have three available to us now!

The Islands are indeed different now. I make no predictions about the future. The ten weeks of the occupation changed our streets, our homes and our environment.

And out in Camp, where the changes wrought by war are less evident, there are certain fields and pastures which are also different now. They contain the graves of some of the soldiers who died in the Falklands War, buried near where they fell in battle. They lie here, among the people they freed, and we are grateful.

Epilogue

I came to the Falklands because that was where I believed God wanted me to be; it was the fulfilment of a lifelong desire to serve God abroad. The 'call' was in a prosaic few words: 'able to butcher one's own meat'. We went to the Falklands because we believed that was God's word to me. And we put it to the test, we saw the obstacles disappear, and within three months we were away.

We had no idea what lay ahead. If in 1979 we could have foreseen the events of 1982, we would have been astonished, because our vision of the future didn't include armed hostilities. But through that experience, God has taught us lessons which he sent us to the Islands to learn.

Before the invasion, I was a methodical person. I expected to know what I would be doing at any given part of the day. I liked to organise my time properly.

The events of the occupation taught me not to fuss in this way, but to be sensitive to what God wanted me to do and the way in which the Lord wanted to lead me.

This became so exciting to me that I would leave the house in the morning, throw my hands in the air, and say: 'Well, Lord; where are we going today?' The day wasn't organised or prepared. I was free to live